Houghton
Mifflin
Harcourt

CALIFORNIA
MATH
Expressions
Common Core

Dr. Karen C. Fuson

GRADE

5

Volume 1

This material is based upon work supported by the
National Science Foundation
under Grant Numbers
ESI-9816320, REC-9806020, and RED-935373.

Any opinions, findings, and conclusions, or recommendations expressed in this material
are those of the author and do not necessarily reflect the views of the National Science Foundation.

VOLUME 1 CONTENTS

UNIT 1 Addition and Subtraction with Fractions

UNIT 2 Addition and Subtraction with Decimals

© Houghton Mifflin Harcourt Publishing Company

UNIT 3 Multiplication and Division with Fractions

UNIT 4 Multiplication with Whole Numbers and Decimals

Student Resources

Family Letter

Content Overview

Dear Family,

Your child is learning about fraction concepts. Using fraction bars, students learn about unit fractions, or fractions that are just one part of the whole, such as $\frac{1}{2}$ or $\frac{1}{4}$.

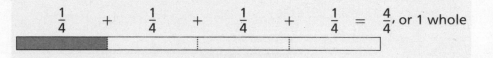

$$\frac{1}{4} \quad + \quad \frac{1}{4} \quad + \quad \frac{1}{4} \quad + \quad \frac{1}{4} \quad = \quad \frac{4}{4}, \text{ or 1 whole}$$

Non-unit fractions are sums of unit fractions.

Unit fractions are used to convert mixed numbers, which have a whole-number part and a fraction part, to fractions in which the top number (numerator) is larger than the bottom number (denominator).

$$\frac{3}{4} = \frac{1}{4} + \frac{1}{4} + \frac{1}{4}$$

$$2\frac{1}{4} = \frac{4}{4} + \frac{4}{4} + \frac{1}{4} = \frac{9}{4}$$

Fraction bars help students understand how to compare, add, and subtract fractions with like denominators.

$$\frac{a}{d} + \frac{b}{d} = \frac{a+b}{d}$$

$$\frac{1}{4} + \frac{2}{4} = \frac{3}{4}$$

$$\frac{a}{d} - \frac{b}{d} = \frac{a-b}{d}$$

$$\frac{3}{4} - \frac{1}{4} = \frac{2}{4}$$

If $a > b$, then

$$\frac{1}{a} < \frac{1}{b} \text{ and } \frac{a}{d} > \frac{b}{d}$$

$$\frac{1}{3} < \frac{1}{2} \text{ and } \frac{3}{7} > \frac{2}{7}$$

These skills extend to fractions with unlike denominators. We rewrite each fraction with a common denominator, using multiplication to make an equivalent fraction.

$$\overset{\times 5}{\underset{\times 5}{\frac{1}{3} = \frac{5}{15}}}$$

We add and subtract mixed numbers by treating the whole-number part and the fraction part separately, ungrouping 1 whole, if needed.

$$\begin{array}{r} 4\frac{1}{3} \\ -2\frac{7}{15} \\ \hline \end{array} = \begin{array}{r} 3\frac{20}{15} \\ 4\frac{5}{15} \\ 2\frac{7}{15} \\ \hline 1\frac{13}{15} \end{array}$$

Sincerely,
Your child's teacher

 CA CC

Unit 1 addresses the following standards from the *Common Core State Standards for Mathematics with California Additions*: **5.NF.1** and **5.NF.2**, and all Mathematical Practices.

© Houghton Mifflin Harcourt Publishing Company

Estimada familia:

Su niño está aprendiendo conceptos de fracciones. Al usar barras de fracciones, los estudiantes aprenden acerca de fracciones unitarias es decir, fracciones que son solo una parte del entero, como $\frac{1}{2}$ ó $\frac{1}{4}$.

$$\frac{1}{4} \quad + \quad \frac{1}{4} \quad + \quad \frac{1}{4} \quad + \quad \frac{1}{4} \quad = \quad \frac{4}{4} \text{ ó 1 entero}$$

Las fracciones que no son unitarias son sumas de fracciones unitarias.

$$\frac{3}{4} = \frac{1}{4} + \frac{1}{4} + \frac{1}{4}$$

Las fracciones unitarias se usan para convertir números mixtos, los cuales tienen una parte formada por un número entero y una parte formada por una fracción, a fracciones en las que el número de arriba (numerador) es mayor que el número de abajo (denominador).

$$2\frac{1}{4} = \frac{4}{4} + \frac{4}{4} + \frac{1}{4} = \frac{9}{4}$$

Las barras de fracciones ayudan a los estudiantes a comprender cómo se comparan, se suman y se restan las fracciones con denominadores iguales:

$$\frac{a}{d} + \frac{b}{d} = \frac{a+b}{d}$$

$$\frac{1}{4} + \frac{2}{4} = \frac{3}{4}$$

$$\frac{a}{d} - \frac{b}{d} = \frac{a-b}{d}$$

$$\frac{3}{4} - \frac{1}{4} = \frac{2}{4}$$

$a > b$ así que

$$\frac{1}{a} < \frac{1}{b} \text{ y } \frac{a}{d} > \frac{b}{d}$$

$$\frac{1}{3} < \frac{1}{2} \text{ y } \frac{3}{4} > \frac{2}{4}$$

Estas destrezas se aplican también a fracciones con denominadores distintos. Volvemos a escribir cada fracción con un denominador común, usando la multiplicación para obtener una fracción equivalente.

$$\begin{array}{c} \times 5 \\ \frac{1}{3} = \frac{5}{15} \\ \times 5 \end{array}$$

Sumamos y restamos números mixtos tratando la parte del número entero y la parte de la fracción por separado, desagrupando 1 entero si es necesario.

$$3\frac{20}{15}$$

$$4\frac{1}{3} = 4\frac{\cancel{5}}{15}$$

$$-2\frac{7}{15} = 2\frac{7}{15}$$
$$\overline{1\frac{13}{15}}$$

Atentamente,
El maestro de su niño

© Houghton Mifflin Harcourt Publishing Company

CA CC

En la Unidad 1 se aplican los siguientes estándares auxiliares, contenidos en los *Estándares estatales comunes de matemáticas con adiciones para California*: **5.NF.1**, **5.NF.2** y todos los de prácticas matemáticas.

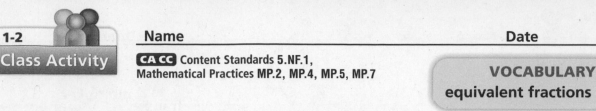

Name   Date

CA CC Content Standards 5.NF.1,
Mathematical Practices MP.2, MP.4, MP.5, MP.7

VOCABULARY
equivalent fractions

▶ Find Equivalent Fractions by Multiplying

You can use a number line to find **equivalent fractions**.

Circle the unit fractions up to $\frac{2}{3}$. Complete the number lines and equation boxes to find equivalent fractions for $\frac{2}{3}$.

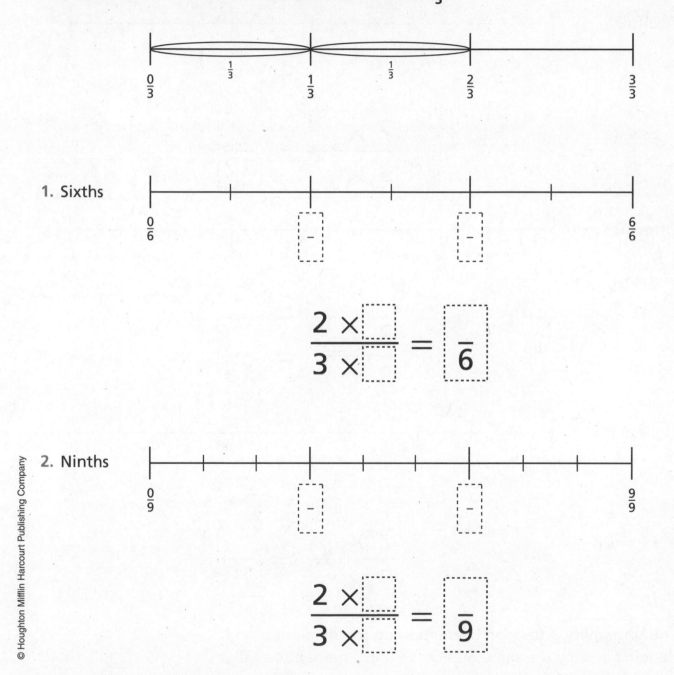

1. Sixths

$$\frac{2 \times \boxed{}}{3 \times \boxed{}} = \boxed{\frac{}{6}}$$

2. Ninths

$$\frac{2 \times \boxed{}}{3 \times \boxed{}} = \boxed{\frac{}{9}}$$

VOCABULARY
multiplier
unsimplify

▶ Find Equivalent Fractions by Multiplying (continued)

Circle the unit fractions up to $\frac{2}{3}$. Complete the number lines and equation boxes to find equivalent fractions for $\frac{2}{3}$.

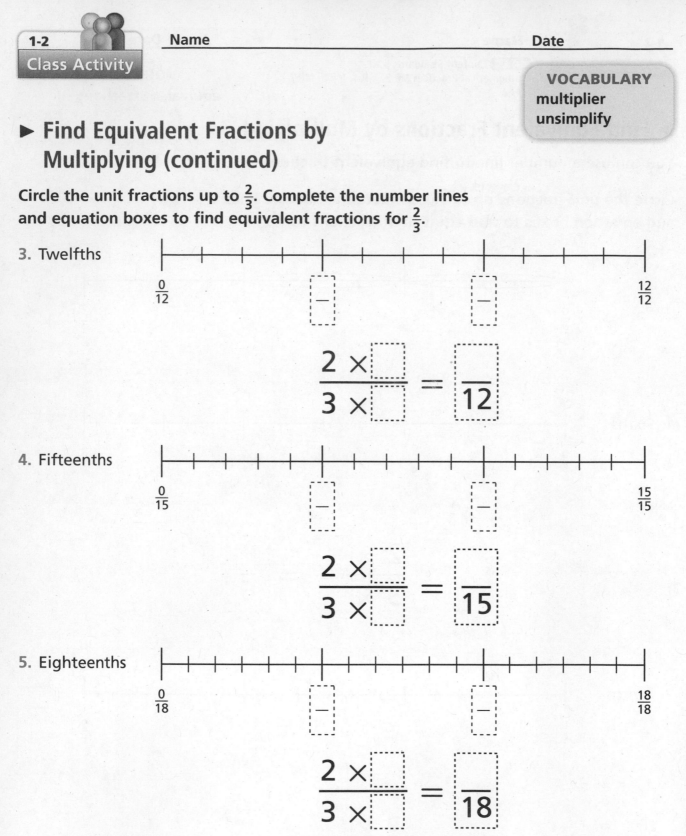

3. Twelfths

$\frac{0}{12}$ ... $\frac{\Box}{\Box}$ ... $\frac{\Box}{\Box}$ ... $\frac{12}{12}$

$$\frac{2 \times \Box}{3 \times \Box} = \frac{\Box}{12}$$

4. Fifteenths

$\frac{0}{15}$ ... $\frac{\Box}{\Box}$ ... $\frac{\Box}{\Box}$ ... $\frac{15}{15}$

$$\frac{2 \times \Box}{3 \times \Box} = \frac{\Box}{15}$$

5. Eighteenths

$\frac{0}{18}$ ... $\frac{\Box}{\Box}$ ... $\frac{\Box}{\Box}$ ... $\frac{18}{18}$

$$\frac{2 \times \Box}{3 \times \Box} = \frac{\Box}{18}$$

6. You **unsimplify** a fraction by multiplying the numerator and denominator by the same number to make more but smaller unit fractions. The number you multiply both parts of the fraction by is called the **multiplier**. Discuss how you unsimplified $\frac{2}{3}$ in Exercises 1–5. What was the multiplier in each exercise?

▶ Find Equivalent Fractions by Dividing

Complete the number lines and equation boxes to show how to **simplify** each fraction to $\frac{2}{3}$.

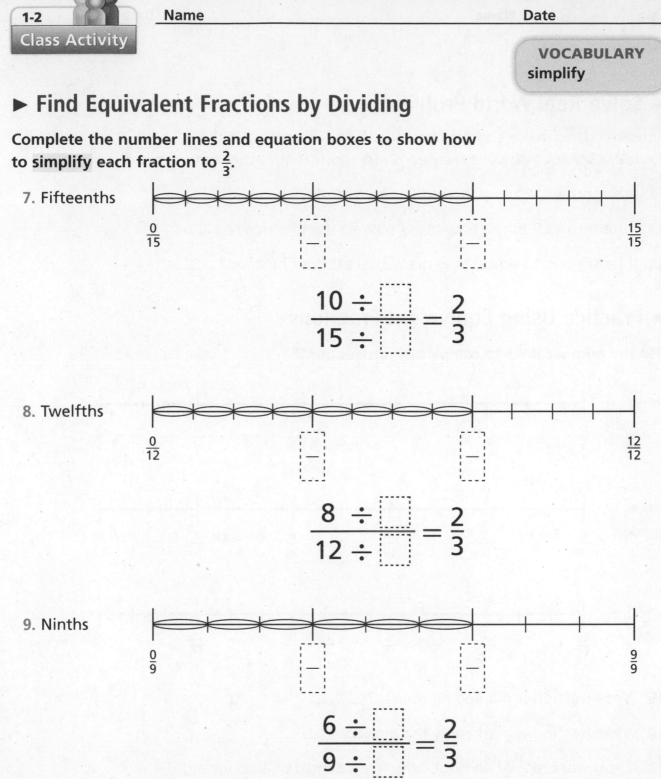

7. Fifteenths

$$\frac{10 \div \square}{15 \div \square} = \frac{2}{3}$$

8. Twelfths

$$\frac{8 \div \square}{12 \div \square} = \frac{2}{3}$$

9. Ninths

$$\frac{6 \div \square}{9 \div \square} = \frac{2}{3}$$

10. When you simplify to make an equivalent fraction, you divide the numerator and denominator by the same number to make fewer but bigger unit fractions. Discuss how that has happened for Exercises 7 through 9 above.

11. Discuss how simplifying and unsimplifying are alike and different.

▶ Solve Real World Problems

Henri needs to make $\frac{2}{3}$ of his free throws in order to make the basketball team. Answer Exercises 12–14 about Henri's throws.

12. If he throws 12 times, how many baskets does he need? _____

13. If he throws 9 times, how many baskets does he need? _____

14. If he throws 15 times, how many baskets does he need? _____

▶ Practice Using Equivalent Fractions

Use the number lines to complete Exercises 15–18.

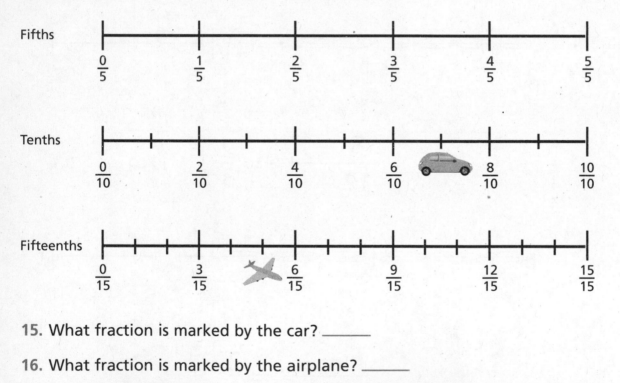

Fifths

$\frac{0}{5}$ $\frac{1}{5}$ $\frac{2}{5}$ $\frac{3}{5}$ $\frac{4}{5}$ $\frac{5}{5}$

Tenths

$\frac{0}{10}$ $\frac{2}{10}$ $\frac{4}{10}$ $\frac{6}{10}$ $\frac{8}{10}$ $\frac{10}{10}$

Fifteenths

$\frac{0}{15}$ $\frac{3}{15}$ $\frac{6}{15}$ $\frac{9}{15}$ $\frac{12}{15}$ $\frac{15}{15}$

15. What fraction is marked by the car? _____

16. What fraction is marked by the airplane? _____

17. If you worked $\frac{4}{5}$ of an hour, how many tenths of an hour did you work?

_____

18. Which is greater, $\frac{2}{5}$ or $\frac{4}{15}$? How do you know?

_____

Explain Equivalent Fractions

▶ Use the Multiplication Table to Find Equivalent Fractions

You can use these multiplication tables to find equivalent fractions.

×	1	2	3	4	5	6	7	8	9	10
1	1	2	3	4	5	6	7	8	9	10
2	2	4	6	8	10	12	14	16	18	20
3	3	6	9	12	15	18	21	24	27	30
4	4	8	12	16	20	24	28	32	36	40
5	5	10	15	20	25	30	35	40	45	50
6	6	12	18	24	30	36	42	48	54	60
7	7	14	21	28	35	42	49	56	63	70
8	8	16	24	32	40	48	56	64	72	80
9	9	18	27	36	45	54	63	72	81	90
10	10	20	30	40	50	60	70	80	90	100

×	1	2	3	4	5	6	7	8	9	10
1	1	2	3	4	5	6	7	8	9	10
2	2	4	6	8	10	12	14	16	18	20
3	3	6	9	12	15	18	21	24	27	30
4	4	8	12	16	20	24	28	32	36	40
5	5	10	15	20	25	30	35	40	45	50
6	6	12	18	24	30	36	42	48	54	60
7	7	14	21	28	35	42	49	56	63	70
8	8	16	24	32	40	48	56	64	72	80
9	9	18	27	36	45	54	63	72	81	90
10	10	20	30	40	50	60	70	80	90	100

$$\frac{3}{5} \quad \frac{6}{10} \quad \frac{9}{15} \quad \frac{12}{20} \quad \frac{15}{25} \quad \frac{18}{30} \quad \frac{21}{35} \quad \frac{24}{40} \quad \frac{27}{45} \quad \frac{30}{50}$$

$$\frac{4}{7} \quad \frac{8}{14} \quad \frac{12}{21} \quad \frac{16}{28} \quad \frac{20}{35} \quad \frac{24}{42} \quad \frac{28}{49} \quad \frac{32}{56} \quad \frac{36}{63} \quad \frac{40}{70}$$

1. Color rows 4 and 9 in the first table. Use the table to complete the equivalent fractions for $\frac{4}{9}$.

   $\frac{4}{9}$ = ____ = ____ = ____ = ____ = ____ = ____ = ____ = ____ = ____

2. Color rows 3 and 8 in the second table. Use the table to complete the equivalent fractions for $\frac{3}{8}$.

   $\frac{3}{8}$ = ____ = ____ = ____ = ____ = ____ = ____ = ____ = ____ = ____

Complete these equivalent fractions.

3. $\frac{1}{4}$ = ____ = ____ = ____ = ____ = ____ = ____ = ____ = ____ = ____

4. $\frac{1}{3}$ = ____ = ____ = ____ = ____ = ____ = ____ = ____ = ____ = ____

© Houghton Mifflin Harcourt Publishing Company

▶ Split Fraction Bars

Use the fraction bars to find equivalent fractions for $\frac{3}{4}$.

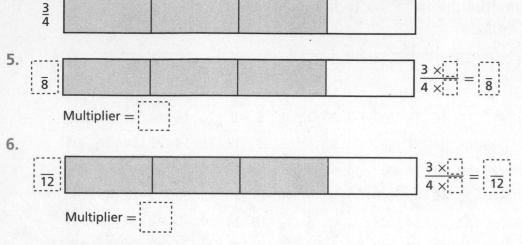

$\frac{3}{4}$

5. $\frac{}{8}$

Multiplier = ⬚

$\dfrac{3 \times \boxed{}}{4 \times \boxed{}} = \dfrac{\boxed{}}{8}$

6. $\frac{}{12}$

Multiplier = ⬚

$\dfrac{3 \times \boxed{}}{4 \times \boxed{}} = \dfrac{\boxed{}}{12}$

▶ What's the Error?

Dear Math Students,

I tried to find a fraction equivalent to $\frac{5}{6}$.
I multiplied the denominator by 2 to make
smaller unit fractions. This can't be right
because $\frac{5}{6}$ is almost 1, and $\frac{5}{12}$ is less than $\frac{1}{2}$.
Why doesn't my method work?

Your friend,
Puzzled Penguin

$\dfrac{5}{6 \times 2} = \dfrac{5}{12}$

7. Write a response to Puzzled Penguin.

_____

_____

_____

_____

_____

Name _____ Date _____

CA CC Content Standards 5.NF.1,
Mathematical Practices MP.2, MP.5, MP.6, MP.7, MP.8

VOCABULARY
greater than, >
less than, <
unit fraction

▶ Like Denominators or Like Numerators

The **greater than** symbol, >, and the **less than** symbol, <, show
how two numbers compare.

$27 < 72$ Twenty-seven is less than seventy-two.

$10 > 3 + 4$ Ten is greater than three plus four.

In this lesson, you'll use these symbols for fraction comparisons.

Same Denominator If two fractions have the same denominator,
then they are made from **unit fractions** of the same size.
The fraction with more unit fractions is greater.

Example: $\frac{3}{5} < \frac{4}{5}$

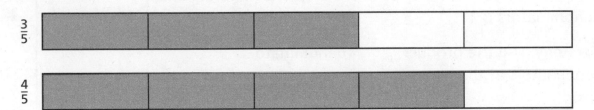

Same Numerator If two fractions have the same numerator,
then the number of unit fractions is the same. The fraction
with the larger unit fractions is greater.

Example: $\frac{2}{5} > \frac{2}{7}$

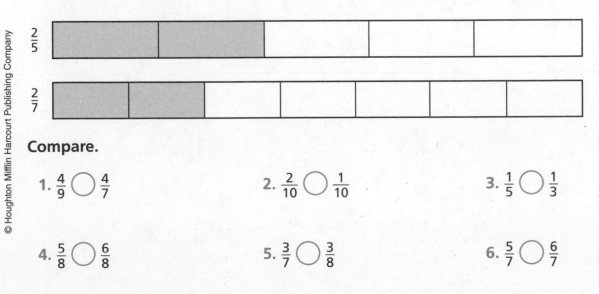

Compare.

1. $\frac{4}{9} \bigcirc \frac{4}{7}$ 2. $\frac{2}{10} \bigcirc \frac{1}{10}$ 3. $\frac{1}{5} \bigcirc \frac{1}{3}$

4. $\frac{5}{8} \bigcirc \frac{6}{8}$ 5. $\frac{3}{7} \bigcirc \frac{3}{8}$ 6. $\frac{5}{7} \bigcirc \frac{6}{7}$

Name _____   **Date** _____

► Unlike Denominators

If two fractions have different denominators, you can compare them by first rewriting them as equivalent fractions with a **common denominator**. You can use different strategies to do this, depending on how the denominators are related.

Case 1: One denominator is a factor of the other. **Possible Strategy:** Use the greater denominator as the common denominator.	**Example:** Compare $\frac{3}{4}$ and $\frac{5}{8}$. Use 8 as the common denominator. $\frac{3 \times 2}{4 \times 2} = \frac{6}{8}$ $\frac{6}{8} > \frac{5}{8}$, so $\frac{3}{4} > \frac{5}{8}$.
Case 2: The only number that is a factor of both denominators is 1. **Possible Strategy:** Use the product of the denominators as the common denominator.	**Example:** Compare $\frac{4}{5}$ and $\frac{5}{7}$. Use 5×7, or 35, as the common denominator. $\frac{4 \times 7}{5 \times 7} = \frac{28}{35}$ $\frac{5 \times 5}{7 \times 5} = \frac{25}{35}$ $\frac{28}{35} > \frac{25}{35}$, so $\frac{4}{5} > \frac{5}{7}$.
Case 3: There is a number besides 1 that is a factor of both denominators. **Possible Strategy:** Use a common denominator that is less than the product of the denominators.	**Example:** Compare $\frac{7}{9}$ and $\frac{5}{6}$. 18 is a common multiple of 9 and 6. Use 18 as the common denominator. $\frac{7 \times 2}{9 \times 2} = \frac{14}{18}$ $\frac{5 \times 3}{6 \times 3} = \frac{15}{18}$ $\frac{14}{18} < \frac{15}{18}$, so $\frac{7}{9} < \frac{5}{6}$.

Compare.

7. $\frac{1}{5} \bigcirc \frac{2}{7}$ 8. $\frac{15}{18} \bigcirc \frac{5}{6}$ 9. $\frac{3}{8} \bigcirc \frac{5}{12}$

10. $\frac{1}{5} \bigcirc \frac{3}{20}$ 11. $\frac{5}{8} \bigcirc \frac{3}{5}$ 12. $\frac{3}{10} \bigcirc \frac{2}{8}$

Name   Date

▶ Special Cases

You can *always* compare two fractions by rewriting them so they have the same denominator. However, in some special cases, you can compare the fractions more efficiently just by using reasoning.

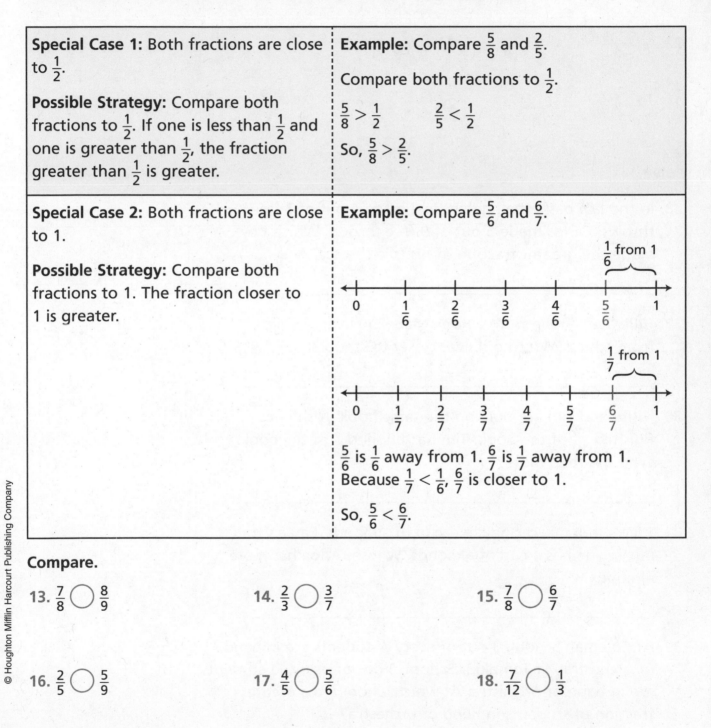

Special Case 1: Both fractions are close to $\frac{1}{2}$. **Possible Strategy:** Compare both fractions to $\frac{1}{2}$. If one is less than $\frac{1}{2}$ and one is greater than $\frac{1}{2}$, the fraction greater than $\frac{1}{2}$ is greater.	**Example:** Compare $\frac{5}{8}$ and $\frac{2}{5}$. Compare both fractions to $\frac{1}{2}$. $\frac{5}{8} > \frac{1}{2}$ $\qquad$ $\frac{2}{5} < \frac{1}{2}$ So, $\frac{5}{8} > \frac{2}{5}$.
Special Case 2: Both fractions are close to 1. **Possible Strategy:** Compare both fractions to 1. The fraction closer to 1 is greater.	**Example:** Compare $\frac{5}{6}$ and $\frac{6}{7}$. $\frac{5}{6}$ is $\frac{1}{6}$ away from 1. $\frac{6}{7}$ is $\frac{1}{7}$ away from 1. Because $\frac{1}{7} < \frac{1}{6}$, $\frac{6}{7}$ is closer to 1. So, $\frac{5}{6} < \frac{6}{7}$.

Compare.

13. $\frac{7}{8} \bigcirc \frac{8}{9}$

14. $\frac{2}{3} \bigcirc \frac{3}{7}$

15. $\frac{7}{8} \bigcirc \frac{6}{7}$

16. $\frac{2}{5} \bigcirc \frac{5}{9}$

17. $\frac{4}{5} \bigcirc \frac{5}{6}$

18. $\frac{7}{12} \bigcirc \frac{1}{3}$

► Mixed Practice

Compare.

19. $\frac{4}{5}$ ◯ $\frac{2}{3}$ 20. $\frac{9}{12}$ ◯ $\frac{6}{8}$ 21. $\frac{7}{9}$ ◯ $\frac{7}{10}$

22. $\frac{2}{3}$ ◯ $\frac{5}{6}$ 23. $\frac{5}{9}$ ◯ $\frac{3}{7}$ 24. $\frac{9}{10}$ ◯ $\frac{8}{9}$

25. $\frac{1}{5}$ ◯ $\frac{2}{9}$ 26. $\frac{3}{8}$ ◯ $\frac{1}{3}$ 27. $\frac{7}{10}$ ◯ $\frac{4}{5}$

Solve.
                                                         Show your work.

28. In the last basketball game, Joel made 4 out of 7 free throws. Carlos made 5 out of 9 free throws. Which boy made the greater fraction of his free throws?

_____

29. Julie lives $\frac{3}{8}$ mile from school. Madeline lives $\frac{5}{12}$ mile from school. Which girl lives closer to school?

_____

30. Nisha and Tim are reading the same book. Nisha has finished $\frac{9}{10}$ of the book. Tim has finished $\frac{8}{9}$ of the book. Who has read more?

_____

31. Julio's trail mix recipe has $\frac{2}{3}$ cup of almonds. Paula's trail mix recipe has $\frac{3}{4}$ cup of almonds. Whose recipe has more almonds?

_____

32. At Coleman School, 3 out of every 7 students are in band or orchestra. At Tompkins School, 5 out of every 11 students are in band or orchestra. At which school are a greater fraction of students in band or orchestra?

_____

1-5

Class Activity

Name _____ **Date** _____

CA CC Content Standards 5.NF.1,
Mathematical Practices MP.3, MP.4, MP.6

VOCABULARY
mixed number

► Change Mixed Numbers to Fractions

A **mixed number** is a number with a whole number part and a fraction part. For example, $2\frac{1}{2}$ is a mixed number. It means 2 *and* $\frac{1}{2}$, or 2 *plus* $\frac{1}{2}$. Mixed numbers can be rewritten as fractions.

Example: $2\frac{1}{2} = 2 + \frac{1}{2} = 1 + 1 + \frac{1}{2} = \frac{2}{2} + \frac{2}{2} + \frac{1}{2} = \frac{5}{2}$

Change each mixed number to a fraction.

1. $3\frac{2}{5} =$ _____

2. $2\frac{3}{8} =$ _____

3. $1\frac{7}{10} =$ _____

4. $4\frac{1}{4} =$ _____

5. $2\frac{5}{9} =$ _____

6. $1\frac{1}{25} =$ _____

► Change Fractions to Mixed Numbers

Any fraction greater than 1 can be rewritten as a mixed number.

Example: $\frac{13}{4} = \frac{4}{4} + \frac{4}{4} + \frac{4}{4} + \frac{1}{4} = 1 + 1 + 1 + \frac{1}{4} = 3\frac{1}{4}$

Change each fraction to a mixed number.

7. $\frac{10}{7} =$ _____

8. $\frac{12}{5} =$ _____

9. $\frac{8}{3} =$ _____

10. $\frac{15}{4} =$ _____

11. $\frac{39}{6} =$ _____

12. $\frac{51}{10} =$ _____

© Houghton Mifflin Harcourt Publishing Company

▶ Real World Problems

13. Jonah ran around a $\frac{1}{4}$-mile track 15 times. Express the distance he ran as a mixed number.

_____

14. A guidance counselor has $2\frac{3}{6}$ hours to meet with students. If she meets with each student for $\frac{1}{6}$ hour, how many students can she see?

_____

▶ What's the Error?

Dear Math Students,

I had to write $3\frac{4}{5}$ as a fraction as part of my homework. I think that $3\frac{4}{5}$ means 3 four-fifths. This is what I wrote:

$$3\frac{4}{5} = \frac{4}{5} + \frac{4}{5} + \frac{4}{5} = \frac{12}{5}$$

My friend told me this is not correct. What did I do wrong? Can you explain how I can write $3\frac{4}{5}$ as a fraction?

Your friend,
Puzzled Penguin

15. Write a response to Puzzled Penguin.

_____

_____

_____

_____

_____

▶ Practice Adding Mixed Numbers

Add. Write each total as a mixed number or a whole number.

1. $4\frac{1}{9} + 2\frac{1}{9}$ 2. $5\frac{3}{8} + 2\frac{2}{8}$ 3. $1\frac{1}{6} + 3\frac{4}{6}$

4. $4\frac{1}{3} + 6\frac{1}{3}$ 5. $2\frac{1}{4} + 2\frac{3}{4}$ 6. $3\frac{2}{7} + 2\frac{5}{7}$

7. $1\frac{3}{5} + 2\frac{4}{5}$ 8. $40\frac{6}{7} + 22\frac{5}{7}$ 9. $6\frac{8}{9} + 4\frac{7}{9}$

▶ Practice Subtracting Mixed Numbers

Subtract. Write the difference as a mixed number or a whole number.

10. $3\frac{2}{3} - 1\frac{1}{3}$ 11. $5\frac{1}{6} - 3\frac{5}{6}$ 12. $2\frac{3}{4} - 1\frac{3}{4}$

13. $4 - 2\frac{3}{8}$ 14. $15\frac{7}{9} - 10\frac{5}{9}$ 15. $12\frac{2}{5} - 8\frac{4}{5}$

▶ Solve Real World Problems

Write an equation. Then solve.

16. A bag contained $6\frac{2}{3}$ cups of flour. Scout used $2\frac{1}{3}$ cups to make some bread. How much flour was left in the bag after she made the bread?

_____

17. Tami and Ty were partners on a science project. Tami worked $4\frac{1}{4}$ hours on the project, and Ty worked $1\frac{3}{4}$ hours. How much time did they spend on the project in all?

_____

▶ Solve Real World Problems (continued)

18. Maryl measures her height very precisely. Last month, she was $56\frac{7}{8}$ inches tall. This month she is $\frac{3}{8}$ inch taller. How tall is she this month?

_____

19. Maryl (from Problem 18) measured her younger brother on January 1 of this year and found that he was $40\frac{3}{16}$ inches tall. On January 1 of last year, he was $37\frac{15}{16}$ inches tall. How much did he grow in a year's time?

_____

▶ What's the Error?

Dear Math Students,

This is a problem from my math homework. My teacher says my answer is not correct, but I can't figure out what I did wrong. Can you help me find and fix my mistake?

Your friend,
Puzzled Penguin

$$5\frac{7}{5}$$
$$\cancel{5\frac{2}{5}}$$
$$-3\frac{4}{5}$$
$$\overline{2\frac{3}{5}}$$

20. Write a response to Puzzled Penguin.

_____

_____

_____

_____

_____

► Use Models to Choose a Denominator

To add two fractions, they must have a common denominator.

Use the models to help you rewrite each sum so the fractions have a common denominator. Below the model, show how to find the equivalent fractions numerically.

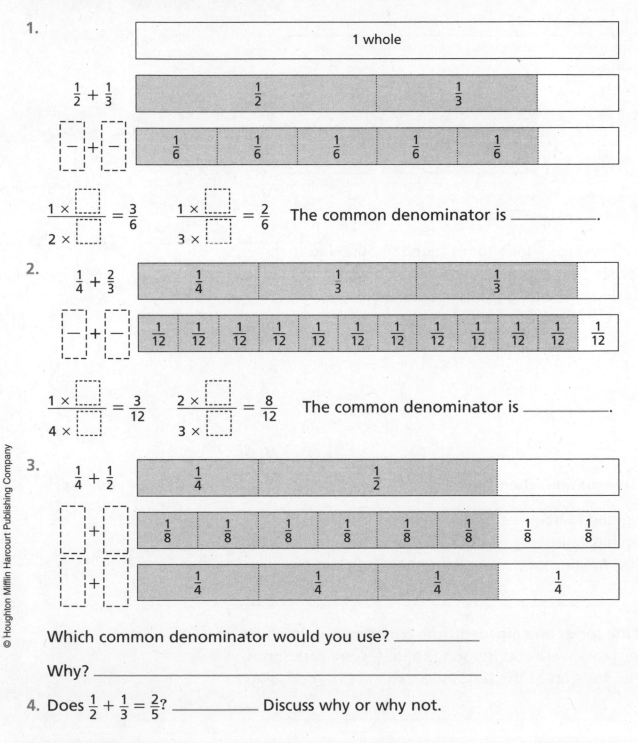

1.

$\frac{1}{2} + \frac{1}{3}$

1 whole

| $\frac{1}{2}$ | $\frac{1}{3}$ | |

$\square$ + $\square$

| $\frac{1}{6}$ | $\frac{1}{6}$ | $\frac{1}{6}$ | $\frac{1}{6}$ | $\frac{1}{6}$ | |

$\dfrac{1 \times \square}{2 \times \square} = \dfrac{3}{6}$ $\dfrac{1 \times \square}{3 \times \square} = \dfrac{2}{6}$ The common denominator is _____.

2.

$\frac{1}{4} + \frac{2}{3}$

| $\frac{1}{4}$ | $\frac{1}{3}$ | $\frac{1}{3}$ | |

$\square$ + $\square$

| $\frac{1}{12}$ | $\frac{1}{12}$ | $\frac{1}{12}$ | $\frac{1}{12}$ | $\frac{1}{12}$ | $\frac{1}{12}$ | $\frac{1}{12}$ | $\frac{1}{12}$ | $\frac{1}{12}$ | $\frac{1}{12}$ | $\frac{1}{12}$ | $\frac{1}{12}$ |

$\dfrac{1 \times \square}{4 \times \square} = \dfrac{3}{12}$ $\dfrac{2 \times \square}{3 \times \square} = \dfrac{8}{12}$ The common denominator is _____.

3.

$\frac{1}{4} + \frac{1}{2}$

| $\frac{1}{4}$ | $\frac{1}{2}$ | |

$\square$ + $\square$

| $\frac{1}{8}$ | $\frac{1}{8}$ | $\frac{1}{8}$ | $\frac{1}{8}$ | $\frac{1}{8}$ | $\frac{1}{8}$ | $\frac{1}{8}$ | $\frac{1}{8}$ |

$\square$ + $\square$

| $\frac{1}{4}$ | $\frac{1}{4}$ | $\frac{1}{4}$ | $\frac{1}{4}$ |

Which common denominator would you use? _____

Why? _____

4. Does $\frac{1}{2} + \frac{1}{3} = \frac{2}{5}$? _____ Discuss why or why not.

▶ Choose a Common Denominator

Rewrite the addition problem so the fractions
have a common denominator. Then find the sum.

5. $\frac{7}{10} + \frac{1}{5} =$ _____ = _____

6. $\frac{3}{11} + \frac{1}{2} =$ _____ = _____

7. $\frac{1}{6} + \frac{3}{4} =$ _____ = _____

8. $\frac{3}{8} + \frac{2}{5} =$ _____ = _____

9. $\frac{3}{10} + \frac{4}{15} =$ _____ = _____

10. $\frac{1}{4} + \frac{5}{8} =$ _____ = _____

11. Bashir walked $\frac{1}{4}$ mile to his friend's house and then
   another $\frac{3}{8}$ mile to the park. Make a diagram to help
   you find the total distance he walked.

Write an equation. Then solve.

Show your work.

12. Meg and Marcus are making a latch-hook rug. So far,
   Meg has finished $\frac{2}{5}$ of the rug, and Marcus has finished $\frac{1}{4}$.
   What fraction of the rug have they completed?

   _____

13. Of the songs downloaded from a music web site on
   Tuesday, $\frac{1}{6}$ were country songs and $\frac{3}{10}$ were rock songs.
   What fraction of the songs were country or rock songs?

   _____

Add Unlike Fractions

▶ Compare and Subtract

Solve.   *Show your work.*

1. Amie used $\frac{7}{9}$ yard of ribbon in her dress. Jasmine
   used $\frac{5}{6}$ yard of ribbon in her dress.

   Which girl used more ribbon? _____

   How much more did she use? _____

2. Mr. Su and Mr. Franks are in the same book club.
   Mr. Su is $\frac{5}{7}$ of the way through this month's
   book. Mr. Franks is $\frac{3}{5}$ of the way through the book.

   Who has read more of the book? _____

   How much more has he read? _____

3. Rami's glass is $\frac{1}{2}$ full. Will's glass is $\frac{3}{8}$ full.

   Whose glass is fuller? _____

   How much fuller is it? _____

▶ Subtraction Practice

Subtract.

4. $\frac{1}{2} - \frac{1}{5}$ 5. $\frac{3}{4} - \frac{1}{8}$ 6. $\frac{9}{10} - \frac{4}{15}$

7. $\frac{1}{3} - \frac{2}{9}$ 8. $\frac{5}{6} - \frac{3}{4}$ 9. $\frac{3}{5} - \frac{1}{4}$

10. $\frac{4}{7} - \frac{1}{8}$ 11. $\frac{5}{8} - \frac{1}{6}$ 12. $\frac{11}{15} - \frac{3}{5}$

► **Mixed Practice**

Add or subtract.

13. $\frac{11}{12} - \frac{5}{12}$

14. $\frac{1}{4} + \frac{5}{12}$

15. $\frac{2}{3} - \frac{5}{9}$

16. $\frac{2}{5} + \frac{1}{3}$

17. $\frac{1}{4} - \frac{5}{32}$

18. $\frac{5}{6} - \frac{2}{9}$

19. $\frac{2}{7} + \frac{5}{7}$

20. $\frac{9}{16} - \frac{5}{24}$

21. $\frac{1}{7} - \frac{1}{8}$

Circle the greater fraction. Then write and solve a subtraction problem to find the difference of the fractions.

22. $\frac{4}{5}$ $\frac{8}{9}$ _____

23. $\frac{3}{10}$ $\frac{2}{5}$ _____

24. $\frac{1}{6}$ $\frac{3}{20}$ _____

Solve.

25. Bette has $\frac{2}{5}$ pound of trail mix. Johnna has $\frac{3}{8}$ pound of trail mix.

    Who has more trail mix? _____

    How much more does she have? _____

26. If Bette and Johnna from Problem 25 combine their trail mix, will they have more or less than $\frac{3}{4}$ pound? Explain.

    _____

    _____

Name _____   Date _____

CA CC Content Standards 5.NF.1, 5.NF.2
Mathematical Practices MP.1, MP.4, MP.7, MP.8

▶ Share Solutions

Add or subtract. Show your work.

1. $2\frac{3}{8}$
    $-\ 1\frac{1}{4}$

2. $4\frac{1}{5}$
    $+\ 2\frac{1}{3}$

3. $7\frac{5}{6}$
    $-\ 3\frac{1}{4}$

4. $6\frac{2}{3}$
    $+\ 4\frac{3}{4}$

5. $4\frac{1}{3}$
    $-\ 2\frac{7}{15}$

6. $9\frac{1}{6}$
    $-\ 5\frac{7}{9}$

▶ Add and Subtract Mixed Numbers

Add or subtract. Show your work.

7. $5\frac{2}{5}$
    $-\ 3\frac{7}{10}$

8. $8\frac{1}{4}$
    $+\ 2\frac{4}{5}$

9. $7\frac{1}{8}$
    $-\ 4\frac{5}{12}$

10. $6\frac{8}{12}$
    $-\ 3\frac{1}{6}$

11. $5\frac{5}{6}$
    $+\ 2\frac{5}{9}$

12. 3
    $-\ 1\frac{7}{11}$

13. $5\frac{5}{8}$
    $+\ 3\frac{5}{12}$

14. $7\frac{1}{10}$
    $-\ 2\frac{3}{5}$

15. $4\frac{1}{5}$
    $-\ 3\frac{1}{3}$

► Solve Word Problems

Write an equation. Then solve.   *Show your work.*

16. Dora the elephant used to eat $2\frac{3}{4}$ tons of food each
    month. Now she is on a diet and eats only $1\frac{7}{8}$ tons.
    By how many tons was Dora's food decreased each month?

    _____

17. Daisy the elephant can reach a branch $10\frac{5}{6}$ feet off the
    ground. Leroy, the tallest elephant, can reach a branch
    $1\frac{1}{2}$ feet higher than this. How high can Leroy reach?

    _____

18. Speedy, the fastest elephant, can run $25\frac{1}{10}$ miles per
    hour. Squirt can run only $10\frac{3}{5}$ miles per hour. How
    many fewer miles can Squirt run in an hour than Speedy?

    _____

Name all the possible pairs.

19. The truck that carries the elephants holds 10 tons.
    Which two elephants could travel together in the truck?

Dora	$5\frac{3}{4}$ tons
Leroy	$6\frac{1}{2}$ tons
Daisy	$4\frac{2}{3}$ tons
Speedy	$5\frac{2}{3}$ tons
Squirt	$3\frac{2}{3}$ tons

_____

_____

Name _____   **Date** _____

CA CC Content Standards 5.NF.1, 5.NF.2, 5.MD.2
Mathematical Practices MP.6, MP.7, MP.8

▶ Choose How to Rename Fractions

The equations in each group have something in common.

Complete each equation.

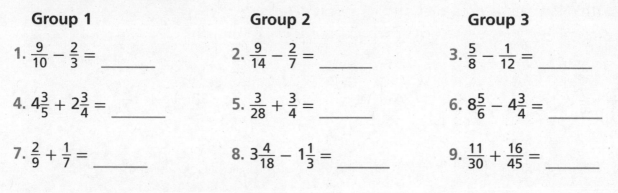

Group 1	Group 2	Group 3
1. $\frac{9}{10} - \frac{2}{3} = $ _____	2. $\frac{9}{14} - \frac{2}{7} = $ _____	3. $\frac{5}{8} - \frac{1}{12} = $ _____
4. $4\frac{3}{5} + 2\frac{3}{4} = $ _____	5. $\frac{3}{28} + \frac{3}{4} = $ _____	6. $8\frac{5}{6} - 4\frac{3}{4} = $ _____
7. $\frac{2}{9} + \frac{1}{7} = $ _____	8. $3\frac{4}{18} - 1\frac{1}{3} = $ _____	9. $\frac{11}{30} + \frac{16}{45} = $ _____

10. Look at the problems in Group 1.

   a. What do the problems in Group 1 have in common?
      (Hint: Focus on the denominators.)

      _____

   b. Describe a strategy for finding a common denominator
      for problems of this type.

      _____

11. Look at the problems in Group 2.

   a. What do the problems in Group 2 have in common?

      _____

   b. Describe a strategy for finding a common denominator
      for problems of this type.

      _____

12. Look at the problems in Group 3.

   a. What do the problems in Group 3 have in common?

      _____

   b. Describe a strategy for finding a common denominator
      for problems of this type.

      _____

▶ Practice Adding and Subtracting

Add or subtract.

13. $6\frac{3}{4} - 4\frac{1}{2}$

14. $4\frac{2}{9} + 1\frac{2}{3}$

15. $3\frac{3}{10} - 1\frac{3}{4}$

16. $2\frac{7}{8} + \frac{7}{8}$

17. $4 - 1\frac{3}{7}$

18. $1\frac{3}{5} + 1\frac{4}{7}$

19. $\frac{7}{9} + \frac{5}{6}$

20. $3\frac{1}{6} - 1\frac{1}{7}$

21. $8\frac{7}{12} + 7\frac{3}{4}$

22. $2 + \frac{1}{8} - 1\frac{1}{3}$

23. $45\frac{33}{100} + 54\frac{7}{10}$

24. $5\frac{1}{12} - 2\frac{4}{9}$

Use the line plot for Problems 25 and 26.

Every week, Mr. Park asks for 1 pound of potato salad at the deli. The line plot shows the actual weight of the salad the deli worker has given him for the past several weeks.

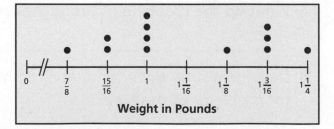

Weight in Pounds

25. What is the difference between the greatest and least weights shown on this graph?

_____

26. For three of the weeks, Mr. Park received less than a pound. What is the combined weight of the salad for these three weeks?

_____

Practice with Unlike Mixed Numbers

CA CC Content Standards 5.NF.1, 5.NF.2
Mathematical Practices MP.3, MP.6

► Estimate Sums and Differences

You can **estimate** the sum or difference of fractions using the **benchmarks** 0, $\frac{1}{2}$, and 1. A number line can help you determine which benchmark each fraction is closest to.

$$\longleftarrow \overset{|}{\underset{0}{\rule{0pt}{1pt}}} \qquad\qquad \overset{|}{\underset{\frac{1}{2}}{\rule{0pt}{1pt}}} \qquad\qquad \overset{|}{\underset{1}{\rule{0pt}{1pt}}} \longrightarrow$$

Use benchmarks of 0, $\frac{1}{2}$, and 1 to estimate the sum or difference. Then find the actual sum or difference.

1. $\frac{1}{4} + \frac{7}{8}$

   Estimate: _____

   Sum: _____

2. $\frac{7}{16} - \frac{5}{12}$

   Estimate: _____

   Difference: _____

3. $\frac{5}{6} + \frac{9}{10}$

   Estimate: _____

   Sum: _____

To estimate the sum or difference of mixed numbers, **round** each mixed number to the nearest whole number or to the nearest half.

Estimate the sum or difference by rounding each mixed number to the nearest whole number. Then find the actual sum or difference.

4. $5\frac{2}{3} - 3\frac{1}{6}$

   Estimate: _____

   Difference: _____

5. $1\frac{1}{4} + 2\frac{7}{10}$

   Estimate: _____

   Sum: _____

6. $3\frac{3}{8} - 1\frac{3}{16}$

   Estimate: _____

   Difference: _____

Use any method you wish to estimate the sum or difference.

7. $10\frac{1}{5} + 5\frac{6}{11}$

   Estimate: _____

   Sum: _____

8. $6\frac{2}{9} - 2\frac{5}{6}$

   Estimate: _____

   Difference: _____

9. $\frac{4}{7} + \frac{7}{9}$

   Estimate: _____

   Sum: _____

10. $\frac{3}{5} - \frac{4}{9}$

    Estimate: _____

    Difference: _____

11. $5\frac{1}{4} + 4\frac{1}{5}$

    Estimate: _____

    Sum: _____

12. $8\frac{4}{5} - 6\frac{1}{8}$

    Estimate: _____

    Difference: _____

Name _____ Date _____

▶ What's the Error?

Dear Math Students,

I got the two answers below marked wrong on my math test.

$$3\frac{1}{4} - 1\frac{7}{8} = 2\frac{3}{8} \qquad \frac{7}{8} + \frac{4}{9} = \frac{11}{17}$$

My friend got 100% on the test. She said she always uses estimation to make sure her answers are reasonable.

Can you explain how I could have used estimation to check my answers?

Your friend,
Puzzled Penguin

13. Write a response to Puzzled Penguin.

_____

_____

_____

_____

_____

▶ Is the Answer Reasonable?

Is the answer reasonable or unreasonable? Explain.

14. $\frac{9}{10} - \frac{2}{5} = 1\frac{3}{10}$

_____

15. $2\frac{4}{5} + 6\frac{1}{6} = 8\frac{29}{30}$

_____

16. $\frac{11}{12} - \frac{7}{8} = \frac{1}{24}$

_____

17. $5\frac{5}{6} + 1\frac{3}{4} = 5\frac{1}{12}$

_____

Reasonable Answers

1-12

Class Activity

Name _____ Date _____

CA CC Content Standards 5.NF.1, 5.NF.2
Mathematical Practices MP.1, MP.3, MP.4, MP.6, MP.7

▶ One-Step Problems

Write an equation and solve the problem. Explain how you know your answer is reasonable.

Show your work.

1. Ariel ran $6\frac{1}{4}$ miles on Saturday. This is $1\frac{3}{4}$ miles more than Harry ran. How far did Harry run?

   Equation and answer: _____

   Why is the answer reasonable?

   _____

   _____

2. After guests drank $4\frac{1}{2}$ gallons of punch, there were $2\frac{5}{8}$ gallons left in the bowl. How much punch was in the bowl to start?

   Equation and answer: _____

   Why is the answer reasonable?

   _____

   _____

3. The beach is $7\frac{1}{3}$ miles from Johanna's house. She walks part of the way. Then she takes the bus the remaining $5\frac{7}{10}$ miles. How far does she walk?

   Equation and answer: _____

   Why is the answer reasonable?

   _____

   _____

4. At a pizza party, the Mehta family ate $1\frac{3}{8}$ pizzas in all. They ate $\frac{9}{12}$ of a cheese pizza and some pepperoni pizza. How much pepperoni pizza did they eat?

   Equation and answer:_____

   Why is the answer reasonable?

   _____

   _____

▶ Problems with More Than One Step

Solve. Explain how you know your answer is reasonable.   *Show your work.*

5. Nora read $\frac{1}{6}$ of a book on Monday and $\frac{2}{5}$ on Tuesday. What fraction of the book does she have left to read?

   Answer: _____

   Why is the answer reasonable?

   _____

   _____

6. A rain barrel contained 32 gallons of water. Bettina used $15\frac{1}{4}$ gallons to water her garden. Then it rained, adding $6\frac{3}{4}$ more gallons. How much water is in the rain barrel now?

   Answer: _____

   Why is the answer reasonable?

   _____

   _____

7. Ana hikes $3\frac{7}{8}$ miles and stops for lunch. Then she hikes $5\frac{1}{4}$ more miles and stops to rest. A sign where she stops says it is $2\frac{1}{2}$ miles to the end of the trail. How long is the trail?

   Answer: _____

   Why is the answer reasonable?

   _____

   _____

8. A pitcher contained 8 cups of juice. The four Alvarez children drank $\frac{2}{3}$ cup, $1\frac{2}{3}$ cups, $1\frac{1}{4}$ cups, and $1\frac{3}{4}$ cups. How much juice is left?

   Answer: _____

   Why is the answer reasonable?

   _____

   _____

▶ Math and Bird Hotels

Have you ever seen a birdhouse? Birdhouses offer birds a place to rest and keep their eggs safe from predators.

Purple martins are birds that nest in colonies. Purple martin birdhouses, like the one at the right, are sometimes called bird hotels.

Suppose that a fifth grade class has decided to build a two-story purple martin bird hotel. Each story of the hotel will have six identical compartments. One story is shown below.

The bird hotel will be made from wood, and each story will have the following characteristics.

▶ The inside dimensions of each compartment measure $7\frac{1}{2}$ in. by $7\frac{1}{2}$ in. by $7\frac{1}{2}$ in.

▶ The wood used for exterior walls is $\frac{5}{8}$-in. thick.

▶ The wood used for interior walls is $\frac{1}{4}$-in. thick.

Calculate the length, width, and height of one story. Do not include a floor or ceiling in your calculations.

1. length _____ in.

2. width _____ in.

3. height _____ in.

Show your work.

► **Math and Bird Hotels (continued)**

The bird hotel will have these additional characteristics.

▸ Each story has a floor that creates an overhang of 1 inch in all directions.

▸ The roof is flat and creates an overhang of 1 inch in all directions.

▸ The wood used for the floors and roof is $\frac{3}{4}$-in. thick.

Calculate the total length, width, and height of the hotel. Include floors and a roof in your calculations.

Show your work.

4. length _____ in.

5. width _____ in.

6. height _____ in.

Purple martins migrate great distances, spending winter in South America and summer in the United States and Canada. A diet of flying insects supplies purple martins with the energy they need to complete such long flights.

Suppose a purple martin migrates about 4,150 miles to South America each fall and about 4,150 miles back to North America each spring. Also suppose the purple martin performs this round trip once each year for three years.

7. At the Equator, the distance around Earth is about 24,900 miles. About how many times around Earth would the purple martin described above fly during its migrations?

_____

Focus on Mathematical Practices

Choose the symbol from the box to compare the fractions.

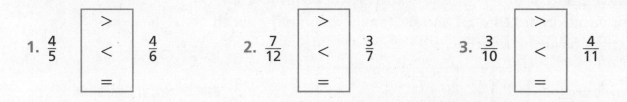

1. $\frac{4}{5}$ $\boxed{\begin{matrix} > \\ < \\ = \end{matrix}}$ $\frac{4}{6}$

2. $\frac{7}{12}$ $\boxed{\begin{matrix} > \\ < \\ = \end{matrix}}$ $\frac{3}{7}$

3. $\frac{3}{10}$ $\boxed{\begin{matrix} > \\ < \\ = \end{matrix}}$ $\frac{4}{11}$

4. Gershon lives $\frac{3}{10}$ mile from the soccer field. How far does Gershon walk if he walks from home to the soccer field and back home?

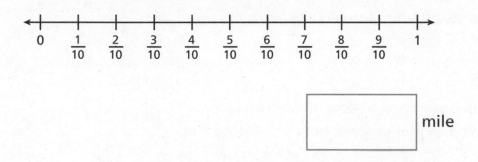

$\boxed{}$ mile

5. Alton shoveled snow on $\frac{4}{6}$ of his driveway before lunch. Then he shoveled $\frac{2}{6}$ of it after lunch. How much more of his driveway did Alton shovel before lunch than after lunch?

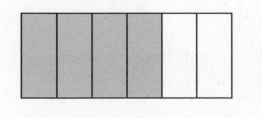

$\boxed{}$

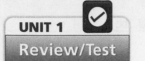

6. Marcus and his family spent $\frac{1}{2}$ of their vacation visiting relatives, and another $\frac{4}{12}$ of it at the beach. What fraction of their vacation did Marcus and his family spend either with relatives or at the beach?

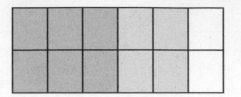

7. Camille uses $4\frac{2}{3}$ yards of white lace and $3\frac{2}{3}$ yards of ivory lace for a craft project.

   Part A

   Write and solve an equation to show how much lace Camille uses. Draw a model to show how you solved the problem.

   Part B

   The project requires a total of $10\frac{2}{3}$ yards of lace. How much more lace does Camille need to finish the project?

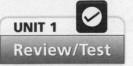
8. Select the fractions that are equivalent to $\frac{3}{4}$. Mark all that apply.

   (A) $\frac{4}{12}$

   (B) $\frac{15}{20}$

   (C) $\frac{23}{24}$

   (D) $\frac{4}{3}$

   (E) $\frac{21}{28}$

   (F) $\frac{33}{44}$

9. Write two fractions that are equivalent to $\frac{8}{12}$. Draw a model with split fraction bars to justify your answer.

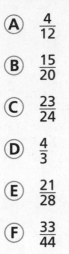

10. Draw a line to match the fraction in the left column with its equivalent mixed number in the right column.

$\frac{11}{4}$ •   • $8\frac{1}{2}$

$\frac{25}{3}$ •   • $2\frac{3}{4}$

$\frac{17}{2}$ •   • $5\frac{3}{5}$

$\frac{28}{5}$ •   • $8\frac{1}{3}$

11. For 11a–11e, choose Yes or No to tell whether the fractions are equivalent.

11a. $\frac{5}{6}$ and $\frac{20}{24}$ ○ Yes   ○ No

11b. $\frac{16}{18}$ and $\frac{8}{9}$ ○ Yes   ○ No

11c. $\frac{12}{22}$ and $\frac{10}{20}$ ○ Yes   ○ No

11d. $\frac{15}{36}$ and $\frac{5}{12}$ ○ Yes   ○ No

11e. $\frac{8}{14}$ and $\frac{8}{28}$ ○ Yes   ○ No

12. For 12a–12d, add or subtract.

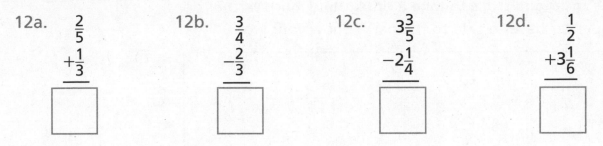

12a. $\dfrac{2}{5}$
    $+\dfrac{1}{3}$

12b. $\dfrac{3}{4}$
    $-\dfrac{2}{3}$

12c. $3\dfrac{3}{5}$
    $-2\dfrac{1}{4}$

12d. $\dfrac{1}{2}$
    $+3\dfrac{1}{6}$

13. Kate pours $\dfrac{3}{4}$ cup of orange juice for herself and another $\dfrac{7}{8}$ cup for her sister. How much orange juice does Kate pour? Show your work.

Write an addition or subtraction equation to solve the word problem using some of the following numbers and symbols. Some numbers are used more than once.

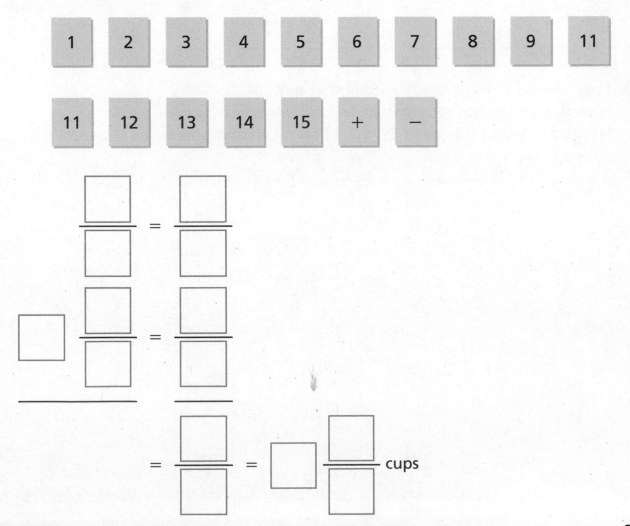

14. Spencer is riding his bicycle $2\frac{7}{10}$ miles to the park. He rides $1\frac{1}{4}$ miles and stops to take a drink. How much farther does Spencer have to ride to the park? Show your work.

15. Eka mixes $6\frac{7}{8}$ pints of grape juice and $4\frac{1}{4}$ pints of cranberry juice to make punch for a party. She has 9 pints of punch left at the end of the party. Estimate how much punch Eka served at the party. Explain how you estimated.

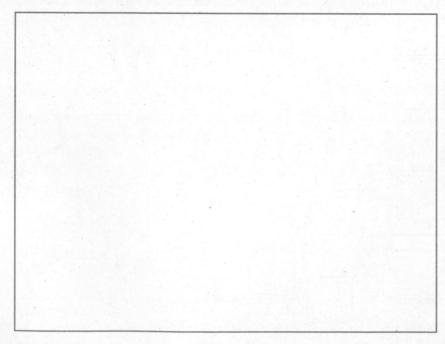

Family Letter

Content Overview

Dear Family,

Your child has studied addition and subtraction with whole numbers and decimals in past years. Unit 2 of *Math Expressions* guides students as they study these topics in greater depth.

The main goals of this unit are:

1. to help students extend their understanding of place value for decimals;

2. to help students add and subtract decimals using the methods they learned previously to add and subtract whole numbers;

3. to develop rounding skills as students estimate sums and differences and engage in graphing activities.

Students will extend and apply their knowledge of place value as they complete activities involving money and metric lengths. When the opportunity arises, ask your child questions about money amounts to help reinforce what is being taught in class.

To accomplish the second goal, students will use various methods of grouping. Students may use whatever method they prefer as long as they understand why it works and can explain it. To add and subtract accurately, students need to align the digits by place value correctly. Observe your child as he or she adds and subtracts. Help align the digits when necessary.

The third goal is accomplished in several ways. Students will learn to use the scale on a graph to understand how to round a number. For example, they see that a number such as 3,879 is between 3,000 and 4,000, but closer to 4,000. So, 3,879 rounded to the nearest thousand is 4,000.

Finally, students will solve real world problems that require estimating sums and differences while adding and subtracting large numbers and decimals.

If you have any questions or comments, please call or write to me.

Sincerely,
Your child's teacher

 CA CC

Unit 2 addresses the following standards from the *Common Core State Standards for Mathematics with California Additions*: **5.NBT.1, 5.NBT.3, 5.NBT.3a, 5.NBT.3b, 5.NBT.4, 5.NBT.7** and all Mathematical Practices.

Estimada familia:

Su niño ha estudiado la suma y resta de números enteros y decimales en años pasados. La Unidad 2 de *Math Expressions* guiará a los estudiantes a medida que estudien esos temas más profundamente.

Los objetivos principales de esta unidad son:

1. ayudar a los estudiantes a ampliar su comprensión del valor posicional de los decimales;

2. ayudar a los estudiantes con la suma y resta de decimales usando los métodos que aprendieron anteriormente para sumar y restar números enteros;

3. desarrollar destrezas de redondeo al estimar sumas y restas y hacer actividades con gráficas.

Los estudiantes ampliarán y aplicarán su conocimiento del valor posicional al realizar actividades con dinero y medidas métricas. Cuando se presente la ocasión, hágale preguntas a su niño sobre cantidades de dinero para reforzar lo que se enseña en la clase.

Los estudiantes lograrán el segundo objetivo utilizando varios métodos de agrupación. Pueden usar el método que prefieran, mientras comprendan por qué funciona y puedan explicarlo. Para sumar y restar con exactitud, necesitan alinear correctamente los dígitos según el valor posicional. Observe a su niño mientras suma y resta. Ayúdele a alinear los dígitos cuando haga falta.

El tercer objetivo se puede cumplir de varias maneras. Los estudiantes aprenderán a usar la escala de una gráfica para comprender cómo se redondea un número. Por ejemplo, van a ver que un número como 3,879 está entre 3,000 y 4,000, pero está más cerca de 4,000. Por lo tanto, redondear 3,879 al millar más cercano da 4,000.

Finalmente, los estudiantes resolverán problemas cotidianos que requieran estimar sumas y restas al sumar y restar números grandes y decimales.

Si tiene alguna pregunta o algún comentario, por favor comuníquese conmigo.

Atentamente,
El maestro de su niño

© Houghton Mifflin Harcourt Publishing Company

CA CC

En la Unidad 2 se aplican los siguientes estándares auxiliares, contenidos en los Estándares estatales comunes de matemáticas con adiciones para California: **5.NBT.1, 5.NBT.3, 5.NBT.3a, 5.NBT.3b, 5.NBT.4, 5.NBT.7** y todos los de prácticas matemáticas.

VOCABULARY
decimal
tenth
hundredth
thousandth

▶ Discuss Fractions and Decimals

Fractions and decimals are special kinds of numbers. They tell the number of equal parts a whole is divided into, and the number of those parts that are being taken or described.

Fraction notation uses a numerator and a denominator to show a whole divided into any number of equal parts.

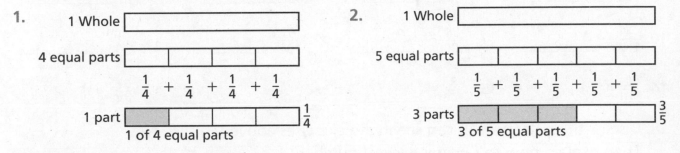

1. 1 Whole

    4 equal parts

    $\frac{1}{4} + \frac{1}{4} + \frac{1}{4} + \frac{1}{4}$

    1 part $\frac{1}{4}$
    1 of 4 equal parts

2. 1 Whole

    5 equal parts

    $\frac{1}{5} + \frac{1}{5} + \frac{1}{5} + \frac{1}{5} + \frac{1}{5}$

    3 parts $\frac{3}{5}$
    3 of 5 equal parts

Decimal notation uses a decimal point to show places to the right of the ones place. The **tenths** place shows 1 whole (such as one dollar) divided into 10 equal parts. The **hundredths** place shows each tenth divided into 10 equal parts.

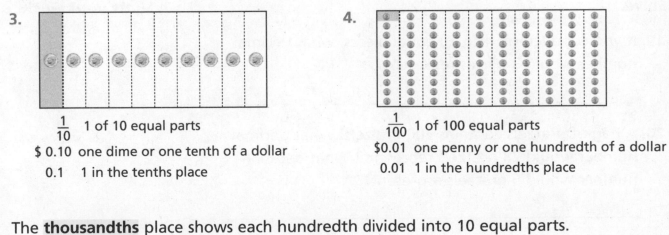

3.

$\frac{1}{10}$ 1 of 10 equal parts

$ 0.10   one dime or one tenth of a dollar

0.1   1 in the tenths place

4.

$\frac{1}{100}$ 1 of 100 equal parts

$0.01   one penny or one hundredth of a dollar

0.01   1 in the hundredths place

The **thousandths** place shows each hundredth divided into 10 equal parts.

5.

$\frac{1}{10}$ of a penny

$\frac{1}{1,000}$ 1 of 1,000 equal parts

$0.001   one tenth of penny or one thousandth of a dollar

0.001   1 in the thousandths place

Name _____   Date _____

▶ Decimals as Equal Parts of Sets

Decimal numbers are read as if they are fractions.
$\frac{37}{100}$ and 0.37 are both said as *thirty-seven hundredths*.

Write each fraction as a decimal number, and then say the number.

6. $\frac{7}{100}$ _____

7. $\frac{16}{100}$ _____

8. $\frac{4}{10}$ _____

9. $\frac{9}{10}$ _____

10. $\frac{5}{1,000}$ _____

11. $\frac{54}{1,000}$ _____

12. $\frac{81}{100}$ _____

13. $\frac{409}{1,000}$ _____

14. $\frac{2}{10}$ _____

15. $\frac{3}{100}$ _____

16. $\frac{16}{1,000}$ _____

17. $\frac{67}{100}$ _____

18. Discuss the patterns you can see in the exercises above. Then explain how to say any decimal number.

_____

_____

Solve.   *Show your work.*

19. If you cut a lemon into 10 equal pieces, what decimal number would 3 pieces represent?

_____

20. A bag of pretzels contains 100 pretzels. What decimal number would 28 pretzels represent? What decimal number would 5 pretzels represent?

_____

21. A beehive is home to 1,000 bees. If 235 bees are out gathering pollen, what decimal number do those bees represent?

_____

22. What decimal number is represented by answering 92 of 100 test questions correctly?

_____

Decimals as Equal Divisions

► Place Value Chart

Discuss the patterns you see in the Place Value Chart below.

← **× 10 (Larger)**   **Place Value Chart**   **÷ 10 (Smaller)** →

Thousands	Hundreds	Tens	ONES	Tenths	Hundredths	Thousandths
1,000.	100.	10.	1.	0.1	0.01	0.001
$\frac{1,000}{1}$	$\frac{100}{1}$	$\frac{10}{1}$	$\frac{1}{1}$	$\frac{1}{10}$	$\frac{1}{100}$	$\frac{1}{1,000}$
$1,000.00	$100.00	$10.00	$1	$0.10	$0.01	$0.001

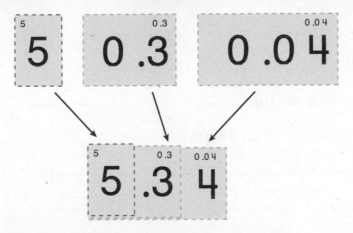

Use your Secret-Code Cards to make numbers on the frame.

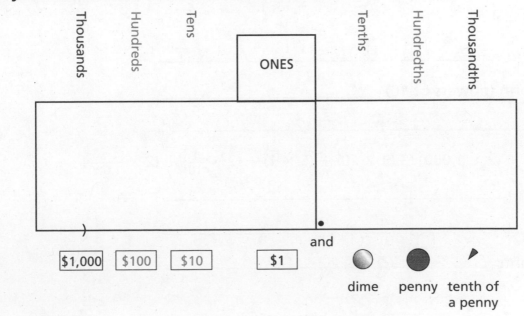

VOCABULARY
standard form
word form
expanded form
powers of 10

▶ Represent Numbers Different Ways

In our place value system, numbers can be expressed different ways. For example, four different ways to represent the number 35.026 are shown below.

standard form	35.026
word form	thirty-five and twenty-six thousandths
expanded form	30 + 5 + 0.02 + 0.006
expanded form (powers of 10)	$(3 \times 10) + (5 \times 1) + (2 \times \frac{1}{100}) + (6 \times \frac{1}{1,000})$

Write each number in three different ways.

1. 12,402

   word form _____

   expanded form _____

   expanded form (powers of 10) _____

2. eight and three hundred five thousandths

   standard form _____

   expanded form _____

   expanded form (powers of 10) _____

3. 70 + 2 + 0.4 + 0.03

   standard form _____

   expanded form (powers of 10) _____

   word form _____

4. $(4 \times 10,000) + (2 \times 1,000) + (3 \times 10) + (5 \times 1) + (2 \times \frac{1}{10}) + (2 \times \frac{1}{1,000})$

   standard form _____

   word form _____

   expanded form _____

▶ Decimal Secret Code Cards

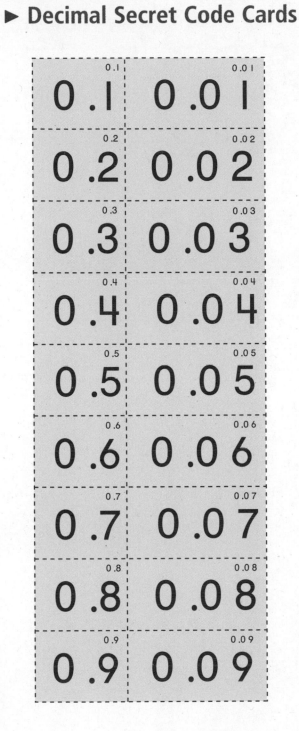

► Decimal Secret Code Cards

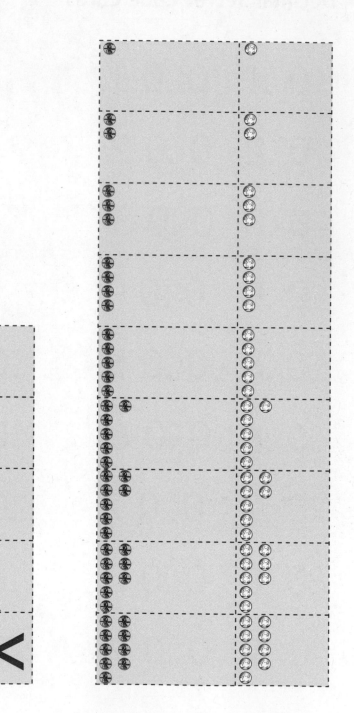

► Decimal Secret Code Cards

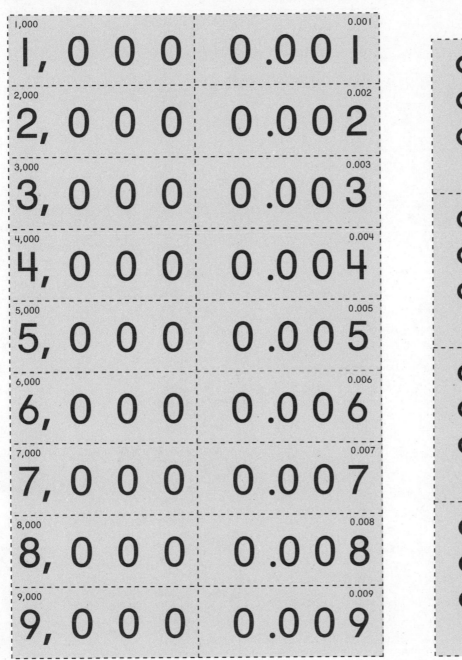

Decimal Secret Code Cards **42C**

► Decimal Secret Code Cards

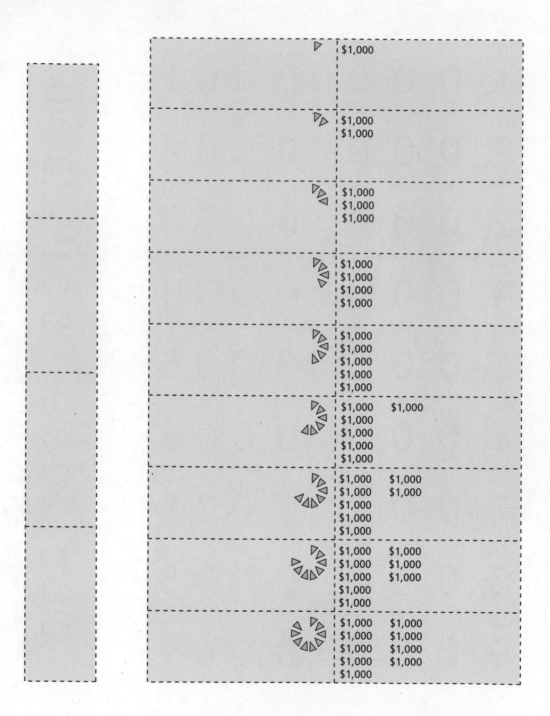

► Secret Code Cards

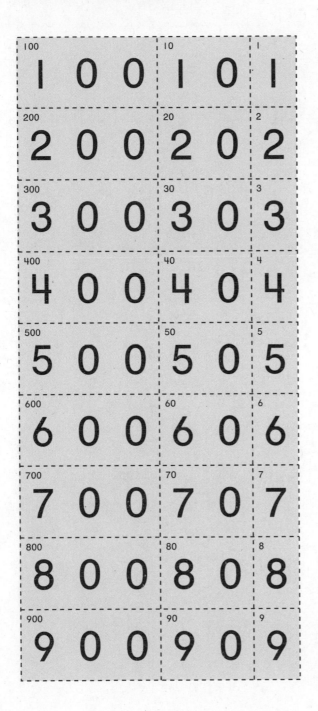

► Secret Code Cards

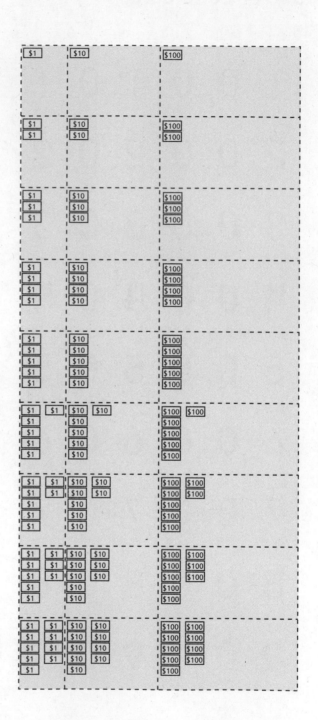

▶ Visualize with Other Models

1. The bar below represents one whole or 1.

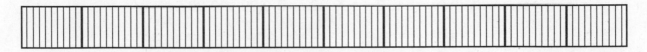

    a. Shade 6 tenths and then shade 2 hundredths.

    b. Discuss Why does the drawing show $0.6 + 0.02 = 0.60 + 0.02 = 0.62$?

2. The number line below is labeled by tenths from 0 to 1.

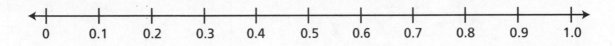

   0   0.1   0.2   0.3   0.4   0.5   0.6   0.7   0.8   0.9   1.0

    a. Begin at 0 and circle a distance to show $0.28 = 0.2 + 0.08 = 0.20 + 0.08$.

    b. Circle a new distance to show $0.74 = 0.7 + 0.04 = 0.70 + 0.04$.

3. Shade the grids to show each amount.

    a. $0.4 = 0.40$ **b.** $0.36 = 0.3 + 0.06$ **c.** 0.001

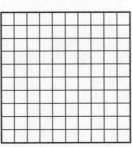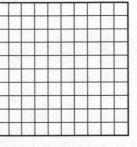

4. Use a sketch of money, a bar representing one whole, a number line, or one or more grids to prove that each statement below is true.

    a. $0.3 = 0.30$ **b.** $0.070 = 0.07$

5. Discuss Equivalent decimals represent the same value. Why does writing zeros to the right of a decimal number not change the value of the number?

▶ Practice Comparisons

We can use Secret-Code Cards to compare decimal numbers.
For example, these cards show that 0.4 > 0.09 and 0.09 > 0.007.

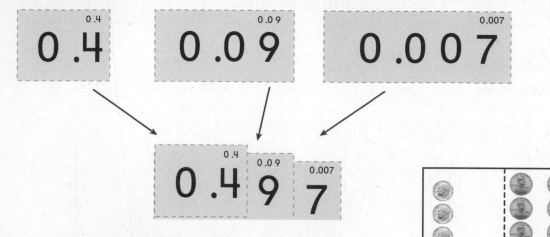

We can also use dimes to represent tenths and
pennies to represent hundredths to show that
the value of a dime is greater than the value
of a penny and the value of a penny is greater
than the value of a tenth of a penny.

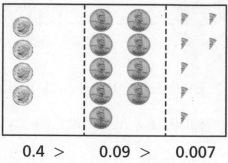

0.4 >   0.09 >   0.007

**Choose any method and use it to complete the following
comparisons. Write >, <, or =.**

6. 0.7 ◯ 0.700   7. 0.070 ◯ 0.07   8. 0.07 ◯ 0.7   9. 0.007 ◯ 0.7

10. 0.8 ◯ 0.62   11. 0.06 ◯ 0.3   12. 0.475 ◯ 0.62   13. 0.3 ◯ 0.29

14. 0.38 ◯ 0.038   15. 0.4 ◯ 0.38   16. 0.38 ◯ 0.380   17. 0.7 ◯ 0.71

18. 0.50 ◯ 0.5   19. 0.21 ◯ 0.2   20. 0.111 ◯ 0.11   21. 0.4 ◯ 0.404

22. Describe a method for comparing decimal numbers.

_____

_____

_____

VOCABULARY
meter (m)
decimeter (dm)
centimeter (cm)
millimeter (mm)

▶ Explore Metric Measures of Length

Use your paper ruler to answer each question.

1. How many decimeters equal one meter? _____

2. How many millimeters equal one centimeter? _____

3. How many millimeters equal one decimeter? _____

4. How many millimeters equal one meter? _____

5. How many centimeters equal one decimeter? _____

6. How many centimeters equal one meter? _____

The last row of the Place Value Chart shows metric measures of length. The most common measurement units are **meter** (m), **decimeter** (dm), **centimeter** (cm), and **millimeter** (mm).

7. Use the meaning of *deci* (one tenth), *centi* (one hundredth), and *milli* (one thousandth) to fill in the right hand side of the chart below.

8. Use the meaning of the Greek words *kilo* (thousand), *hecto* (hundred), and *deka* (ten) to fill in the left side of the chart.

× 10 (Larger) ⟵——————   **Place Value Chart**   ——————⟶ **÷ 10 (Smaller)**

Thousands	Hundreds	Tens	ONES	Tenths	Hundredths	Thousandths
1,000.	100.	10.	1.	0.1	0.01	0.001
$\frac{1,000}{1}$	$\frac{100}{1}$	$\frac{10}{1}$	$\frac{1}{1}$	$\frac{1}{10}$	$\frac{1}{100}$	$\frac{1}{1,000}$
$1,000.00	$100.00	$10.00	$1.00	$0.10	$0.01	$0.001
_____ m kilometer km	_____ m hectometer hm	_____ m dekameter dam	_____ meter m	_____ m decimeter dm	_____ m centimeter cm	_____ m millimeter mm

► Real World Problems with Metric Lengths

Read each measurement below. Say the number of meters, decimeters, centimeters, and millimeters.

For example, 7.284 m is 7 meters, 2 decimeters, 8 centimeters, and 4 millimeters.

9. 7.284 m **10.** 45.132 m **11.** 29.16 m **12.** 304 m **13.** 16.02 m

Write an equation. Then solve

14. Tori had fabric that was 6.2 meters long. She used some and now has 1.45 meters. How much did she use?

_____

15. Matt is competing in the long jump event. His first jump was 3.56 m. So far, the longest jump in the event is 4.02 m. How much farther must Matt jump to be in first place?

_____

16. Patrick ran 53 meters away from Marty and then ran 16.02 meters directly back towards him. How far was Patrick from Marty then?

_____

17. Sarita has some ribbon. After she used 23.8 cm of it, she had 50 cm left. How much ribbon did Sarita start with?

_____

Write your own problems.

18. Write an addition word problem using the measurements in Exercises 11 and 13.

_____

_____

_____

▶ Addition Problems

When adding, remember to align the place values of the numbers.

Dear Math Students,

I am ordering a CD from a catalog. The price of the CD is $15 and the tax is $0.15. Altogether, then, I will have to pay $30 for this CD. The tax makes the cost twice as much! Doesn't this seem unreasonable to you? Or have I made some kind of a mistake?

Your friend,
Puzzled Penguin

1. Write a response to Puzzled Penguin.

_____

_____

_____

_____

_____

Add. Try to solve mentally.

2. $28 + 32¢ = _____   3. $42.05 + 63¢ = _____   4. 56¢ + $8.27 = _____

5. 43 + 0.26 = _____   6. 57.3 + 0.89 = _____   7. 92.17 + 1.6 = _____

8. 4 m + 0.03 m = _____   9. 2.5 m + 0.08 m = _____   10. 6 m + 0.007 m = _____

11. Explain how to add two decimal numbers. Give an example.

_____

_____

▶ Practice

Add each pair of numbers.

12.	4.78	13.	37.56	14.	203.05	15.	$8.59
	+ 5.23		+ 2.78		+ 48.9		+ $0.78

16. 9.53 + 0.7

17. 605.4 + 0.89

18. 0.37 + 0.15

19. 91 + 0.51

20.	876.2	21.	95,238.77	22.	332.28	23.	66,488.82
	+ 5,274.2		+ 78.41		+ 91.36		+ 124,507.09

Write an equation. Then solve.

Show your work.

24. When Bill got his kitten, Missy, she weighed 807.39 grams. She now weighs 1,918.7 grams more than she did when Bill first brought her home. How much does Missy weigh now?

_____

25. Ajit is tracking how much rainfall falls at his house. The first day 1.45 centimeters of rain fell. The second day 2.3 centimeters of rain fell. On the third day, 1.68 centimeters of rain fell. How many centimeters of rain fell in all over the three days?

_____

26. Walt is running for exercise. He ran around Lake Blue and then ran 2.75 miles home. He ran for a total of 4.25 miles. How far did he run around Lake Blue?

_____

▶ Subtraction with Ungrouping

Ungrouping allows you to subtract greater numbers from lesser numbers.

Dear Math Students,

I measured the depth of the snow on my iceberg and it was 40.15 cm deep. Last week the snow was 36.84 cm deep. I subtracted to find out how much it had changed and got a difference of 14.31 cm. That isn't what the meteorologist said. Can you help me find my mistake?

Your friend,
Puzzled Penguin

1. Write a response to Puzzled Penguin.

_____

_____

_____

_____

_____

▶ Practice

Subtract. Use addition to check your answers.

2. 168.75
  − 59.82

3. 6,222.01
    − 48.04

4. 1.09
  − 0.7

5. 100,561.78 − 814.99

6. 0.91 − 0.88

7. 37,000 − 2.73

8. 80,615 − 74,468.63

9. 610,716 − 9.45

10. 909, 015.5 − 90,901.55

▶ Real World Problems

Write an equation. Then solve.

11. One year, the Sahara Desert received 0.79 inches of rain. That same year the rain forest in Brazil received 324 inches. How much more rain fell in the rain forest that year than in the desert?

_____

12. A newborn kangaroo measures about 0.02 meter in height. If the newborn kangaroo grows to be an adult that is 2.7 meters tall, how much will the baby kangaroo have grown?

_____

▶ Practice

Add or subtract.

13. 2,333.56
     + 81.09

14.   0.08
     + 0.97

15. 610,877.50
     − 22,948

16.   24
     − 0.18

17.   555,222
     +178,109.50

18.   9.28
     +1.76

19. 90.44 − 1.37

20. 4,822 − 0.08

21. 667,087.6 + 4,055.75

22. 807 + 3.48

23. 77.08 − 25

24. 2,004 − 5.43

Name _____ **Date** _____

CA CC Content Standards 5.NBT.7
Mathematical Practices MP.6, MP.7, MP.8

VOCABULARY
Commutative Property of Addition
Associative Property of Addition

▶ Practice with Regrouping and Reordering

The **Commutative Property** and **Associative Property**
can help you add.

Properties
Commutative Property of Addition $a + b = b + a$
Associative Property of Addition $(a + b) + c = a + (b + c)$

You can sometimes group or reorder numbers to help you use
mental math more quickly. Explain how you could use the
Commutative and Associative Properties to help you add mentally.

1. 30,000
    20,000 _____
    80,000 _____
    49,000 _____
    + 70,000 _____
    _____

2. 1.500
    1.200 _____
    1.300 _____
    + 1.678 _____
    _____
    _____

3. 5.75
    5.4 _____
    5.25 _____
    5.17 _____
    + 5.6 _____
    _____

4. $\frac{1}{6}$
    $\frac{5}{11}$ _____
    $\frac{3}{4}$ _____
    $\frac{5}{6}$ _____
    $+ \frac{1}{4}$ _____

5. 8 million + 39 million + 2 million

_____

_____

6. 40 hundredths + 8 and 56 hundredths + 60 hundredths

_____

_____

7. $\frac{8}{9} + 5\frac{1}{5} + \frac{1}{9}$

_____

VOCABULARY
Distributative Property of Multiplication over Addition

The **Distributive Property** can also help you compute mentally.

Distributive Property	$a \times (b + c) = (a \times b) + (a \times c)$

Discuss how you could use the Distributive Property to write each problem with only two factors. Then solve the problems mentally.

8. $(7 \times 25) + (7 \times 75) =$ _____

9. $(800 \times 9) + (200 \times 9) =$ _____

10. Use what you know about the Commutative Property to solve for n.
$968.73 + 532.15 = 532.15 + n$

_____

Find each answer by using the Associative Property.

11. $(749 + 600) + 400 =$ _____

12. $3.20 + (2.80 + 1.37) =$ _____

13. Use the Distributive Property to help you find the combined area of these rectangles.

```
        199 cm                          101 cm
10 cm ┌──────────────┐        10 cm ┌──────────────┐
      └──────────────┘              └──────────────┘
```

_____

_____

► Properties and Real World Situations

Which property best describes each situation below: Commutative, Associative, or Distributive?

14. Miranda cannot add ($56.73 + $8.00) + $2.00 very easily. So, she regroups the problem as $56.73 + ($8.00 + $2.00).

15. Brady did not know the answer to 2×403. So, he broke a factor into two addends and multiplied each addend by the other factor. Then, he added the two products together: $(2 \times 400) + (2 \times 3)$.

_____   _____

2-8
Class Activity

Name _____ **Date** _____

CA CC Content Standards 5.NBT.4
Mathematical Practices MP.1, MP.2, MP.3, MP.6, MP.8

VOCABULARY
round

▶ Round Decimal Numbers

Solve.

1. A number changed to 12.6 after it was rounded. To what place was the number rounded? Explain how you know.

_____

_____

2. A number changed to 3.25 after it was rounded. To what place was the number rounded? Explain how you know.

_____

_____

3. A number changed to 193 after it was rounded. To what place was the number rounded? Explain how you know.

_____

_____

Round to the nearest whole number.

4. 31.75 _____   5. 6.49 _____   6. 11.5 _____

7. 0.97 _____   8. 319.1 _____   9. 9.086 _____

Round to the nearest hundredth.

10. 4.051 _____   11. 16.686 _____   12. 0.994 _____

13. 51.202 _____   14. 775.115 _____   15. 4,258.999 _____

Round to the nearest tenth.

16. 51.16 _____   17. 8.55 _____   18. 147.67 _____

19. 0.84 _____   20. 29.20 _____   21. 0.182 _____

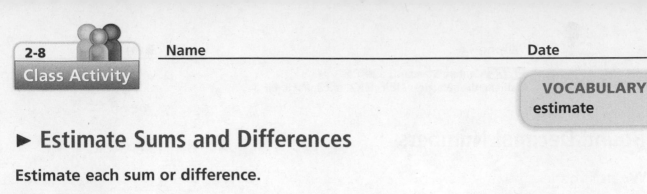

▶ Estimate Sums and Differences

Estimate each sum or difference.

| 22. | $17.25 − $11.79 | 23. | $8.90 + $5.80 | 24. | $3.52 − $1.54 |

| 25. | $6.36 + $6.81 | 26. | 0.716 − 0.698 | 27. | 10.239 + 9.062 |

Solve.

28. Rick thinks the total cost of a $89.95 soccer goal and a $9.99 soccer ball is $90.94. Write your estimate of the total cost; then write the exact cost.

   Estimate _____   Exact Cost _____

   Was Rick's answer reasonable? Explain why or why not.

   _____

29. Marti has 20.15 m of red and blue fabric. Of that, 9.28 m is red, the rest is blue. Marti calculated that she has 10.87 m of blue fabric.

   Is Marti's answer reasonable? Explain why or why not.

   _____

30. In a video racing game, Lee completed one lap in 47.32 seconds. Donna completed one lap in 45.41 seconds.

   Which lap was faster? _____

   How many seconds faster was the lap?

   Estimate _____   Exact Answer _____

   Is your exact answer reasonable? Explain why or why not.

   _____

Name _____ Date _____

CA CC Content Standards 5.NBT.3b, 5.NBT.4
Mathematical Practices MP.1, MP.3, MP.4, MP.6

▶ Graphs with Decimal Numbers

This bar graph shows the length of some common beetles.

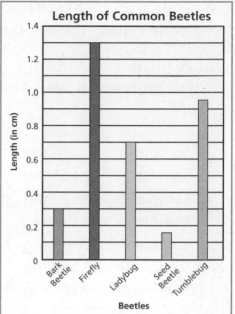

Length of Common Beetles

1. What is the length of a bark beetle?

   _____

2. How much longer is a firefly than a bark beetle?

   _____

3. Estimate the length of a tumblebug in hundredths of a centimeter.

   _____

4. The actual length of one beetle shown is 0.150 centimeters. Which beetle is that?

   _____

5. A June bug is about 2.5 centimeters in length. About how many times as tall as the tumblebug bar would the June bug bar be? (Hint: Round the lengths to whole numbers to help you estimate the height of the June bug's bar.)

   _____

▶ What's the Error?

Dear Math Students,

For the Science Fair, I recorded the heights of several plants a month after I put different fertilizers on them. I made a bar graph of the data. Did I make my graph correctly? If not, how can I fix it?

Your friend,
Puzzled Penguin

Plant Heights After 1 Month

6. Write an answer to Puzzled Penguin.

_____

_____

► Make a Bar Graph with Decimal Numbers

Last week, a chemist kept track of the masses of the different samples he tested. The box on the left shows the information.

7. Use the box on the right to make a list that shows each mass rounded to the nearest hundredth of a milligram.

Sample A 0.136 mg	
Sample B 0.168 mg	
Sample C 0.129 mg	
Sample D 0.117 mg	
Sample E 0.179 mg	
Sample F 0.162 mg	
Sample G 0.109 mg	

Sample A	
Sample B	
Sample C	
Sample D	
Sample E	
Sample F	
Sample G	

8. Which sample had the greatest mass? _____

9. Which sample had the least mass? _____

10. Estimate the total mass of the samples to the nearest tenth. _____

11. Make a bar graph to show these masses rounded to the nearest hundredth.

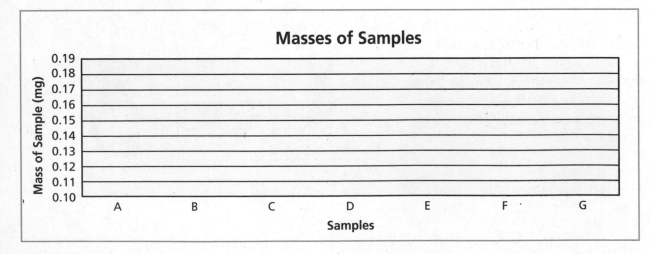

12. Write the samples' masses in order from from least to greatest.

_____

Graphs with Decimal Numbers

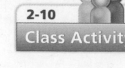

▶ Math and Our Solar System

To describe distances on Earth, you do not need to use units of measure greater than thousands of miles. In space, however, distances are vast, and greater units of measure are used to describe those distances.

Distances between objects in our solar system usually involve many millions of miles.

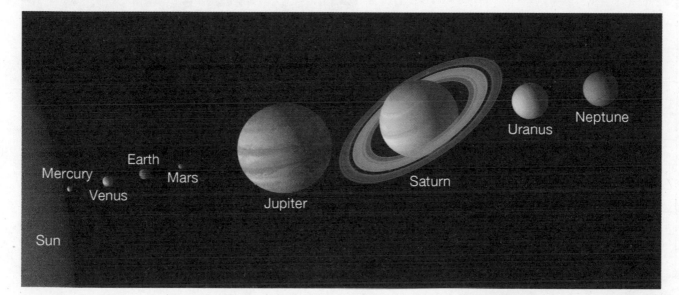

Scientists express the distances in astronomical units (AU). One AU is the distance from the Earth to our Sun, which is about 93 million miles.

$$1 \text{ AU} \approx 93{,}000{,}000 \text{ miles}$$

When you work with distances in our solar system, it is easier to add and subtract astronomical units than it is to add and subtract numbers in the millions.

1 AU

Show your work.

Solve.

1. Venus orbits 0.72 AU from the Sun. Mercury's orbit is 0.33 AU closer. Explain why subtraction is used to find the distance of Mercury's orbit from the Sun. Then find the distance.

_____

_____

The table below shows the distances in astronomical units (AU) of the planets from our Sun. Since the planets Mercury and Venus are closer to the Sun than Earth, their distance from the Sun is less than 1 AU. Outer planets such as Jupiter and Neptune have distances greater than 1 AU.

Planet	Orbital Distance from the Sun (in AU)
Mercury	0.39
Venus	0.72
Earth	1.0
Mars	1.5
Jupiter	5.2
Saturn	9.5
Uranus	19.2
Neptune	30.1

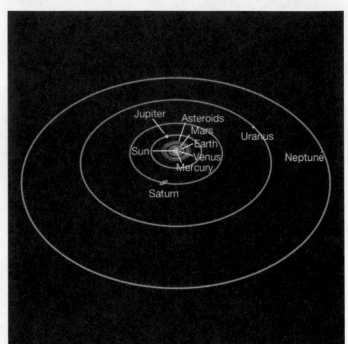

Solve. Compute the distance between the planets' orbits.   *Show your work.*

2. Venus and Earth   _____ AU

3. Earth and Mars   _____ AU

4. Jupiter and Saturn   _____ AU

5. Mercury and Neptune _____ AU

6. Write Mercury's orbital distance (in AU) from the Sun as a fraction.

_____

7. The sum of the orbital distances from the Sun of which four planets is closest to the orbital distance from the Sun to Neptune?

_____

© Houghton Mifflin Harcourt Publishing Company

Focus on Mathematical Practices

1. Use the Associative Property to add. Explain how the Associative Property helps you add mentally.

$$2.57 + 1.7 + 5.3$$

2. Use the Associative Property to add. Show your work.

$$3.25 + (7.75 + 4.89)$$

3. Select the number in which the digit 8 is ten times the value of the digit 8 in 4.381. Mark all that apply.

(A) 183.9   (D) 9.548

(B) 3.458   (E) 0.184

(C) 56.82   (F) 1.83

4. Use the numbers and decimal to write a number in which the digit 2 is one tenth the value of the digit 2 in 8.524.

_____

5. Write 247.903 in expanded form.

6. Write seventeen thousand and one hundred six thousandths in standard form.

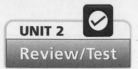
7. Write 9.57 in word form.

8. Jon is not sure how to write 81.402 in expanded form using powers of ten. Write the number in each box that will correctly complete the expanded form of the number.

$$\left(8 \times \boxed{}\right) + (1 \times 1) + \left(4 \times \boxed{}\right) + \left(2 \times \boxed{}\right)$$

9. Write $(2 \times 100) + (9 \times 1) + \left(7 \times \frac{1}{10}\right) + \left(8 \times \frac{1}{1,000}\right)$ in standard form.

10. In which number is the value of the digit 5 greater? Write the number in the box.

3.514   25   [ ]

11. Select the number that shows the digit 4 with a value of 0.04. Mark all that apply.

(A) 3.104   (D) 145.6

(B) 4.541   (E) 1.743

(C) 8.412   (F) 0.441

Choose the symbol from the box to compare the numbers.

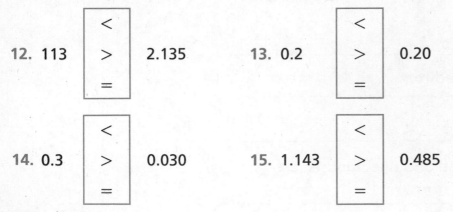

12. 113 [< > =] 2.135   13. 0.2 [< > =] 0.20

14. 0.3 [< > =] 0.030   15. 1.143 [< > =] 0.485

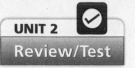
16. Round 17.641 to the nearest whole number.

> [   ]

17. Choose the digits that show 3.096 rounded to the nearest hundredth.

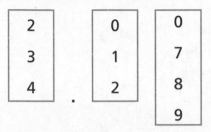

18. Write the letter for the place value in the box next to the number that shows 143.649 rounded to that place value.

(A) tenths

(B) hundreds

(C) ones

(D) tens

(E) hundredths

[   ] 143.65

[   ] 100

[   ] 144

[   ] 143.6

[   ] 140

Add or subtract.

19. 276.25
      + 13.87

20.   4.72
       −3.93

Estimate the sum or difference.

21. $44.31
      − $12.35
      ――――
        $

22. 21.95
       +3.04

> [   ]

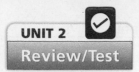
23. The distance around a park is 308.94 meters. Nikki runs around the park twice to catch her dog. How many meters does she run? Explain why your answer is reasonable and draw a model to show how you solved the problem..

24. Rey buys a skateboard for $89.98 and a helmet for $44.85 on tax-free day at a sports store. The store clerk gives Rey a discount of $18.50 for both items. Rey gives the clerk $150. How much change should he receive? Explain why your answer is reasonable.

25. At Bryan's school, the two fastest runners in the 100-yard dash had race times of 12.19 seconds and 12.38 seconds. Estimate and then find how much faster the first place runner was than the second place runner. Explain how you found your answers.

26. For numbers 26a–26e, choose Yes or No to indicate whether the number is correctly rounded to the given place value.

26a. 245.6 rounded to the ones is 246   ○ Yes   ○ No

26b. 723.14 rounded to the hundreds is 720   ○ Yes   ○ No

26c. 1,341.45 rounded to the tens is 134   ○ Yes   ○ No

26d. 45.932 rounded to the tenths is 45.9   ○ Yes   ○ No

26e. 219.934 rounded to the hundredths
is 219.93   ○ Yes   ○ No

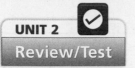

Name _____ Date _____

27. Shayna takes measurements of rainfall for a week. She measures 0.24 centimeters on Monday, 0.32 centimeters on Tuesday, and 0.18 centimeters on Friday. The rest of the days had no rain.

Part A

Complete the data table.

Day	Rainfall (cm)
Sunday	0
Wednesday	0
	0
Saturday	

Part B

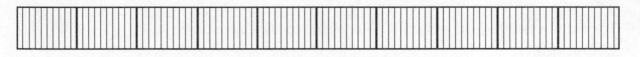

The bar represents one centimeter of rainfall. Shade the bar to show the total rainfall Shayna measured.

28. A lizard's body is 2.45 feet long. The lizard's tail is 1.82 feet long.

Part A

How long is the lizard? _____ feet

Part B

How much longer will the lizard need to grow to be 5 feet long? _____ feet

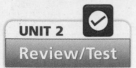
Name _____   Date _____

29. While working at a yard sale, Ying helps a customer who buys items that cost $5, $2, $2.50, and $0.25. The customer hands Ying $3 and says to keep the $0.18 change.

Part A

How much did the customer think the total was? Show your work.

Part B

What mistake did the customer make? Show your work and explain your answer.

30. For numbers 30a–30d, select True or False for the sum or difference.

30a.
$$\begin{array}{r} 2.58 \\ +0.75 \\ \hline 3.33 \end{array}$$
○ True   ○ False

30b.
$$\begin{array}{r} 12.967 \\ +\quad 55 \\ \hline 13.022 \end{array}$$
○ True   ○ False

30c.
$$\begin{array}{r} 12.25 \\ +15.86 \\ \hline 27.01 \end{array}$$
○ True   ○ False

30d.
$$\begin{array}{r} 105.5 \\ +\quad 4.2 \\ \hline 109.7 \end{array}$$
○ True   ○ False

Family Letter

Content Overview

Dear Family,

In this unit of *Math Expressions*, your child is studying multiplication and division with fractions.

Multiplication tells how many times we are taking a number. For example, when we take $\frac{4}{5}$ of something, we multiply it by $\frac{4}{5}$ to find the answer. In this unit, your child will learn to:

- multiply a whole number by a unit fraction

$$\frac{1}{b} \cdot w = \frac{w}{b} \qquad \frac{1}{3} \cdot 5 = \frac{5}{3}$$

- multiply a whole number by a non-unit fraction

$$\frac{a}{b} \cdot w = \frac{a \cdot w}{b} \qquad \frac{2}{3} \cdot 5 = \frac{10}{3}$$

- multiply two fractions

$$\frac{a}{b} \cdot \frac{c}{d} = \frac{a \cdot c}{b \cdot d} \qquad \frac{2}{3} \cdot \frac{5}{7} = \frac{10}{21}$$

Division tells us how many of a certain number are inside another number. For example, when we ask how many times $\frac{1}{5}$ fits inside a number, we divide it by $\frac{1}{5}$ to find out. Using the relationship between multiplication and division, your child will discover how to:

- divide a whole number by a whole number

$$a \div b = a \cdot \frac{1}{b} = \frac{a}{b} \qquad 3 \div 4 = 3 \cdot \frac{1}{4} = \frac{3}{4}$$

- divide a whole number by a unit fraction

$$w \div \frac{1}{d} = w \cdot d \qquad 6 \div \frac{1}{5} = 6 \cdot 5 = 30$$

- divide a unit fraction by a whole number

$$\frac{1}{d} \div w = \frac{1}{d} \cdot \frac{1}{w} \qquad \frac{1}{2} \div 4 = \frac{1}{2} \cdot \frac{1}{4} = \frac{1}{8}$$

Throughout the unit, students will also practice comparing, adding, and subtracting fractions. This helps them maintain what they have learned. It also helps them to see how the various fractional operations are alike and how they are different. It is particularly important for your child to realize that comparing, adding, and subtracting fractions require the denominators to be the same. For multiplying and dividing, this is not true.

If you have any questions about this unit, please call or write to me.

Sincerely,
Your child's teacher

 CA CC

Unit 3 addresses the following standards from the *Common Core State Standards for Mathematics with California Additions:* 5.NF.3, 5.NF.4, 5.NF.4a, 5.NF.4b, 5.NF.5, 5.NF.5a, 5.NF.5b, 5.NF.6, 5.NF.7, 5.NF.7a, 5.NF.7b, 5.NF.7c, and all Mathematical Practices.

Un vistazo general al contenido

Estimada familia:

En esta unidad de *Math Expressions* su niño está estudiando la multiplicación y la división con fracciones.

La multiplicación nos dice cuántas veces se toma un número. Por ejemplo, cuando tomamos $\frac{4}{5}$ de algo, lo multiplicamos por $\frac{4}{5}$ para hallar la respuesta. En esta unidad su niño aprenderá a:

- multiplicar un número entero por una fracción unitaria
$$\frac{1}{b} \cdot w = \frac{w}{b} \qquad \frac{1}{3} \cdot 5 = \frac{5}{3}$$

- multiplicar un número entero por una fracción no unitaria
$$\frac{a}{b} \cdot w = \frac{a \cdot w}{b} \qquad \frac{2}{3} \cdot 5 = \frac{10}{3}$$

- multiplicar dos fracciones
$$\frac{a}{b} \cdot \frac{c}{d} = \frac{a \cdot c}{b \cdot d} \qquad \frac{2}{3} \cdot \frac{5}{7} = \frac{10}{21}$$

La división nos dice cuántas veces cabe un número dentro de otro número. Por ejemplo, cuando preguntamos cuántas veces cabe $\frac{1}{5}$ en un número, dividimos el número entre $\frac{1}{5}$ para saberlo. Al usar la relación entre la multiplicación y la división, su niño va a descubrir cómo:

- dividir un entero entre un entero
$$a \div b = a \cdot \frac{1}{b} = \frac{a}{b} \qquad 3 \div 4 = 3 \cdot \frac{1}{4} = \frac{3}{4}$$

- dividir un entero entre una fracción unitaria
$$w \div \frac{1}{d} = w \times d \qquad 6 \div \frac{1}{5} = 6 \times 5 = 30$$

- dividir una fracción unitaria entre un entero
$$\frac{1}{d} \div w = \frac{1}{d} \times \frac{1}{w} \qquad \frac{1}{2} \div 4 = \frac{1}{2} \times \frac{1}{4} = \frac{1}{8}$$

En esta unidad los estudiantes también practicarán comparaciones, y sumas y restas con fracciones. Esto los ayudará a retener lo que han aprendido. También los ayudará a ver las semejanzas y diferencias entre las operaciones con fracciones. Es importante que su niño se dé cuenta de que para comparar, sumar y restar fracciones, las fracciones deben tener el mismo denominador. Esto no aplica para la multiplicación y división.

Si tiene alguna duda o algún comentario, por favor comuníquese conmigo.

Atentamente,
El maestro de su niño

CA CC

En la Unidad 3 se aplican los siguientes estándares auxiliares, contenidos en los Estándares estatales comunes de matemáticas con adiciones para California: **5.NF.3, 5.NF.4, 5.NF.4a, 5.NF.4b, 5.NF.5, 5.NF.5a, 5.NF.5b, 5.NF.6, 5.NF.7, 5.NF.7a, 5.NF.7b, 5.NF.7c,** y todos los de prácticas matemáticas.

▶ Multiply by a Unit Fraction

Complete.

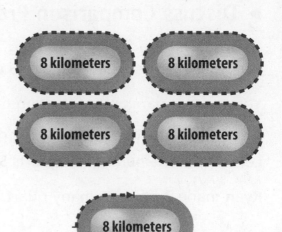

1. A path around a large park is 8 kilometers long. Alex ran around the path 4 times.

   8 taken 4 times = _____ kilometers

   $4 \cdot 8$ = _____ kilometers

2. Kento ran around the same path $\frac{1}{4}$ time.

   8 taken $\frac{1}{4}$ time = _____ kilometers

   $\frac{1}{4} \cdot 8$ = _____ kilometers

3. Markers come in boxes of 6. Alta has 3 boxes.

   6 taken 3 times = _____ markers

   $3 \cdot 6$ = _____ markers

3 groups of 6

4. Isabel has $\frac{1}{3}$ of a box of 6 markers.

   6 taken $\frac{1}{3}$ time = _____ markers

   $\frac{1}{3} \cdot 6$ = _____ markers

$\frac{1}{3}$ **group of 6**

▶ Relate Fraction Multiplication and Whole Number Division

Complete each equation chain like the one shown.

$$\frac{1}{4} \text{ of } 8 \;=\; \frac{1}{4} \cdot 8 \;=\; 8 \div 4 \;=\; \frac{8}{4} \;=\; 2$$

5. $\frac{1}{3}$ of 9 = _____ = _____ = _____ = _____

6. $\frac{1}{7}$ of 21 = _____ = _____ = _____ = _____

7. $\frac{1}{5}$ of 30 = _____ = _____ = _____ = _____

8. Which expression does *not* mean the same thing as the others?

   $\frac{1}{6} \cdot 24$ $24 \div 6$ $\frac{24}{6}$ $\frac{6}{24}$ $\frac{1}{6}$ of 24

Name _____   Date _____

▶ Discuss Comparison Problems

To prepare for a family gathering, Sara and Ryan made soup.
Sara made 2 quarts. Ryan made 6 quarts.

You can compare amounts using multiplication and division.

Let *r* equal the number of quarts Ryan made.
Let *s* equal the number of quarts Sara made.

Ryan made 3 times as many quarts as Sara.

$$r = 3 \cdot s$$

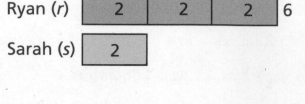

Sara made one third as many quarts as Ryan.

$$s = \frac{1}{3} \cdot r \text{ or } s = r \div 3$$

Solve.

Natasha made 12 quarts of soup. Manuel made 3 quarts.

9. Draw **comparison bars** to show the amount of
   soup each person made.

10. _____ made 4 times as many quarts as _____.

11. _____ made $\frac{1}{4}$ as many quarts as _____.

12. Write two multiplication equations that compare
    the amounts.

    $n = $ _____ $m = $ _____

13. Write a division equation that compares the amounts.

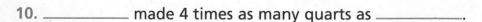

_____

Basic Multiplication Concepts

▶ Solve Comparison Problems

Solve.

In the gym, 8 girls are standing in one line and 4 boys are standing in another line.

14. Draw comparison bars to compare the number of people in each line.

15. Write two multiplication equations that compare the number of girls (g) to the number of boys (b).

    $g =$ _____ $b =$ _____

16. Write a division equation that compares the number of boys (b) to the number of girls (g).

    _____

17. A collection of coins contains 20 pennies and 4 nickels.

    Write two multiplication equations and a division equation that compare the number of pennies (p) and the number of nickels (n).

    _____   _____   _____

18. A fifth-grade class is made up of 12 boys and 24 girls. How many times as many girls as boys are in the class?

    _____

19. Fred has 24 football cards. Scott has $\frac{1}{6}$ as many football cards as Fred. How many football cards does Scott have?

    _____

▶ Compare Data in Graphs and Tables

20. How many times as many fish did Bill catch as Amy?

_____

21. How many times as many fish did Amy catch as Bill?

_____

22. What is $\frac{1}{3} \cdot 15$? What is $15 \div 3$? What is $\frac{15}{3}$?

_____

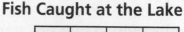

Fish Caught at the Lake

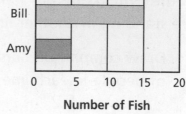

Number of Fish

Write two statements for each pair of players. Use the word *times*.

23. Compare Gina's points and Brent's points.

_____

_____

24. Compare Brent's points and Jacob's points.

_____

_____

25. Compare Jacob's points and Gina's points.

_____

_____

Points at the Basketball Game

Player	Points
Gina	32
Brent	8
Jacob	4

26. Which are the shortest and longest snakes? How do you know?

_____

27. If Speedy is 25 inches long, how long is Lola?

_____

28. If Pretzel is 50 inches long, how long is Speedy? How long is Lola?

_____

Length of Snakes at the Zoo

Snake	Inches
Speedy	n
Lola	$\frac{1}{5} \cdot n$
Pretzel	$5 \cdot n$

Basic Multiplication Concepts

3-2
Class Activity

Name _____ Date _____

CA CC Content Standards 5.NF.4, 5.NF.4a, 5.NF.6,
Mathematical Practices MP.1, MP.4, MP.6, MP.7

▶ Visualize the Separate Steps

Silver City is 24 miles away. Gus has driven $\frac{1}{4}$ of the distance. Emma has driven $\frac{3}{4}$ of the distance.

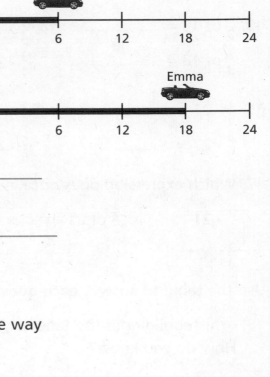

1. How many miles has Gus driven? _____

2. How many miles has Emma driven? _____

3. How many times as far as Gus has Emma driven? _____

4. If $\frac{1}{5}$ of a distance is 3 km, how far is $\frac{4}{5}$? _____

5. If $\frac{1}{8}$ of a container weighs 2 pounds, how many pounds is $\frac{3}{8}$ of the container? _____

6. If $\frac{1}{7}$ of a book is 4 pages, how many pages is $\frac{2}{7}$ of the book? _____

Shady Grove is 40 miles away. Middletown is $\frac{1}{5}$ of the way there and Parkview is $\frac{2}{5}$ of the way.

7. How many miles away is Middletown? _____

8. How many miles away is Parkview? _____

9. Ocean City is 42 miles from home. We have gone 35 miles. What fraction of the distance have we gone? _____

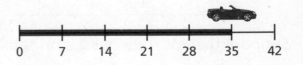

10. Eagle Rock is 72 miles away. When we had gone $\frac{2}{9}$ of the distance, we stopped for gas. How many miles had we traveled? _____

11. Perilous Peak is 80 miles away. We are $\frac{3}{10}$ of the way there. How many more miles do we have to go? _____

12. Windy Bay is 48 miles away. Make up your own fraction word problem with multiplication. Be sure to include a non-unit fraction.

_____

_____

VOCABULARY
factor
product

▶ Practice Multiplication with Fractions

Solve the problem pairs.

13. $\frac{1}{3}$ of 18 = _____   14. $\frac{1}{4} \cdot 32$ = _____

    $\frac{2}{3}$ of 18 = _____ $\frac{3}{4} \cdot 32$ = _____

15. $\frac{1}{9} \cdot 27$ = _____   16. $\frac{1}{6} \cdot 42$ = _____

    $\frac{4}{9} \cdot 27$ = _____ $\frac{5}{6} \cdot 42$ = _____

Parts of a Multiplication Problem

$$\frac{3}{5} \cdot 10 = 6$$

factor   factor   product

17. Which expression does *not* have the same value as the others?

$\frac{2}{3} \cdot 21$ $\frac{2}{3}$ of 21 $\left(\frac{1}{3} \text{ of } 21\right) + \left(\frac{1}{3} \text{ of } 21\right)$

$\frac{2}{3} + 21$ $\frac{21}{3} + \frac{21}{3}$ $\left(\frac{1}{3} \text{ of } 21\right) \cdot 2$

Use the table to answer each question.

18. Which building is the tallest? Which is the shortest? How do you know?

_____

_____

_____

Building	Number of Stories
Bank	n
Bus station	$\frac{1}{6} \cdot n$
Sport shop	$\frac{5}{6} \cdot n$
Hotel	$6 \cdot n$

Suppose the bus station is 2 stories tall.

19. How many stories does the sport shop have? _____

20. How many stories does the bank have? _____

Suppose the bank is 5 stories tall.

21. How many stories tall is the hotel? _____

Suppose the hotel is 36 stories tall.

22. How many stories does the bank have? _____

23. How many stories does the bus station have? _____

24. How many stories does the sport shop have? _____

▶ Model the Product $\frac{1}{d} \cdot w$

Farmer Diaz has 3 acres of land. He plows $\frac{1}{5}$ of this land.
The number of acres he plows is

$\frac{1}{5}$ of 3 or $\frac{1}{5} \cdot 3$

The diagram at the right shows Farmer Diaz's land
divided vertically into 3 acres. The dashed horizontal
segments divide the land into five parts. The shaded
strip is the $\frac{1}{5}$ of the land Farmer Diaz plowed.

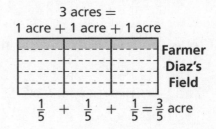

3 acres =
1 acre + 1 acre + 1 acre

Farmer
Diaz's
Field

$\frac{1}{5}$ + $\frac{1}{5}$ + $\frac{1}{5} = \frac{3}{5}$ acre

The drawing shows that taking $\frac{1}{5}$ of the 3 acres is the same as
taking $\frac{1}{5}$ of each acre and combining them. We can show this
mathematically.

$$\frac{1}{5} \cdot 3 = \frac{1}{5}(1 + 1 + 1)$$
$$= \left(\frac{1}{5} \cdot 1\right) + \left(\frac{1}{5} \cdot 1\right) + \left(\frac{1}{5} \cdot 1\right)$$
$$= \frac{1}{5} + \frac{1}{5} + \frac{1}{5}$$
$$= \frac{3}{5}$$

So $\frac{1}{5}$ of the 3 acres is $\frac{3}{5}$ acre.

1. Farmer Smith has 4 acres of land. She plows $\frac{1}{3}$ of
   her land. Divide and shade the drawing at the right
   to show the part of the land she plows.

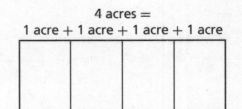

4 acres =
1 acre + 1 acre + 1 acre + 1 acre

2. Express $\frac{1}{3} \cdot 4$ as a sum of unit fractions.

   $\frac{1}{3} \cdot 4 = $ _____

3. What area does Farmer Smith plow? _____

4. Farmer Hanson plows $\frac{1}{7}$ of his 2 acres of land. What area
   does he plow?

   _____

5. Olga walks 9 blocks to school. Her friend Louis walks only $\frac{1}{5}$ of
   that distance. How many blocks does Louis walk to school?

   _____

© Houghton Mifflin Harcourt Publishing Company

▶ Multiply by a Non-Unit Fraction

6. Which expression does *not* have the same value as the others?

$\frac{1}{4}$ of 3 $\frac{1}{4} \cdot 3$ $4 \cdot \frac{1}{3}$ $\frac{1}{4} + \frac{1}{4} + \frac{1}{4}$ $3 \cdot \frac{1}{4}$

Circle the fractions on the number lines to help you multiply.

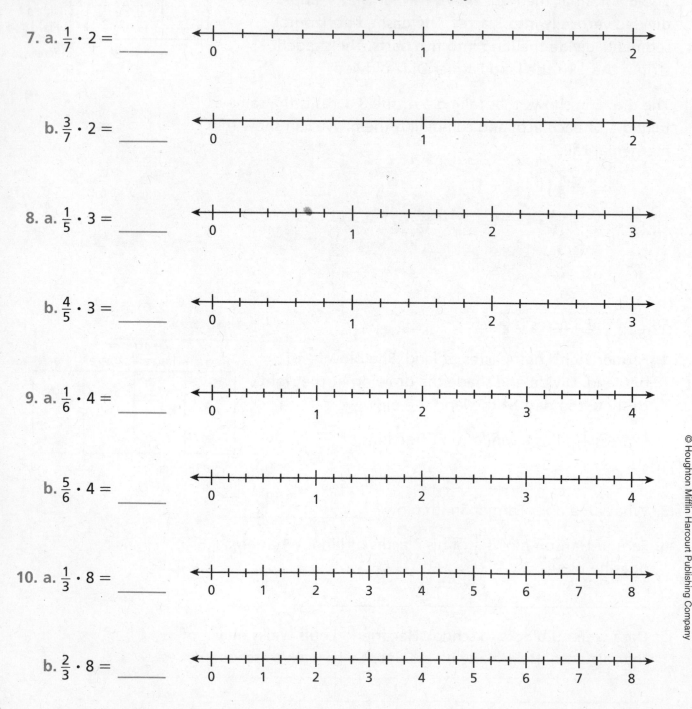

7. a. $\frac{1}{7} \cdot 2 =$ _____

b. $\frac{3}{7} \cdot 2 =$ _____

8. a. $\frac{1}{5} \cdot 3 =$ _____

b. $\frac{4}{5} \cdot 3 =$ _____

9. a. $\frac{1}{6} \cdot 4 =$ _____

b. $\frac{5}{6} \cdot 4 =$ _____

10. a. $\frac{1}{3} \cdot 8 =$ _____

b. $\frac{2}{3} \cdot 8 =$ _____

CA CC Content Standards 5.NF.4, 5.NF.4a, 5.NF.4b, 5.NF.5, 5.NF.6 Mathematical Practices MP.1, MP.2, MP.4, MP.5, MP.6, MP.7

▶ Use Bar Models to Multiply Fractions

Miguel explains how to use fraction bars to find $\frac{2}{3} \cdot \frac{4}{5}$:

First, I circle 4 fifths on the fifths fraction bar.

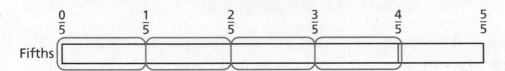

To find $\frac{2}{3}$ of $\frac{4}{5}$, I can circle $\frac{2}{3}$ of each fifth. But, first I have to split each fifth into three parts. After I do this, the bar is divided into fifteenths.

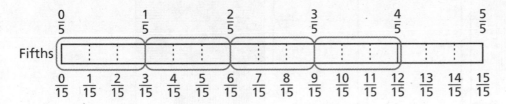

Now, it is easy to circle 2 thirds of each of the 4 fifths.

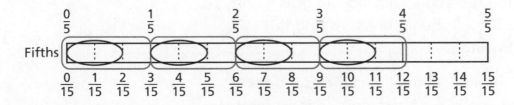

Each group I circled has 2 fifteenths, so I circled 4 groups of 2 fifteenths. That's 8 fifteenths in all. So, $\frac{2}{3} \cdot \frac{4}{5} = \frac{8}{15}$.

1. Use the sixths bar below to model $\frac{3}{4} \cdot \frac{5}{6}$.

   $\frac{3}{4} \cdot \frac{5}{6} =$ _____

   Sixths

2. Use the sevenths bar below to model $\frac{2}{3} \cdot \frac{4}{7}$.

   $\frac{2}{3} \cdot \frac{4}{7} =$ _____

   Sevenths

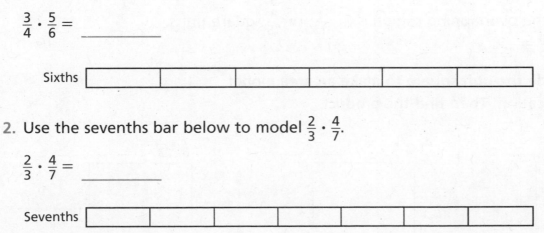

▶ Use Area Models to Multiply Fractions

Jessie knows that the area of a rectangle is its length times its width. She explains how to use this idea to model $\frac{2}{3} \cdot \frac{4}{5}$:

I need to draw a rectangle with side lengths $\frac{2}{3}$ unit and $\frac{4}{5}$ unit.

I start with a unit square and divide it vertically into fifths. Then I shade $\frac{4}{5}$.

Next, I divide the square horizontally into thirds, and shade $\frac{2}{3}$.

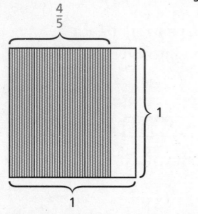

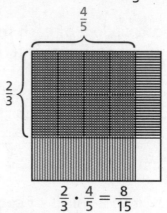

$$\frac{2}{3} \cdot \frac{4}{5} = \frac{8}{15}$$

The overlapping part is a rectangle with side lengths $\frac{2}{3}$ unit and $\frac{4}{5}$ unit. So, its area is $\frac{2}{3} \cdot \frac{4}{5}$ square units. To find this area, I noticed the following:

▶ There are $3 \cdot 5$, or 15, identical small rectangles inside the unit square. Each one is $\frac{1}{15}$ square unit, so it represents the unit fraction $\frac{1}{15}$.

▶ There are $2 \cdot 4$, or 8, of these unit-fraction rectangles inside the $\frac{2}{3}$ by $\frac{4}{5}$ rectangle.

So the area of the overlapping region is $8 \cdot \frac{1}{15}$, or $\frac{8}{15}$ square units. This means $\frac{2}{3} \cdot \frac{4}{5} = \frac{8}{15}$.

Divide and shade the unit square to make an area model for the multiplication. Then find the product.

3. $\frac{1}{2} \cdot \frac{3}{8} =$ _____

4. $\frac{3}{4} \cdot \frac{2}{3} =$ _____

5. $\frac{5}{6} \cdot \frac{1}{3} =$ _____

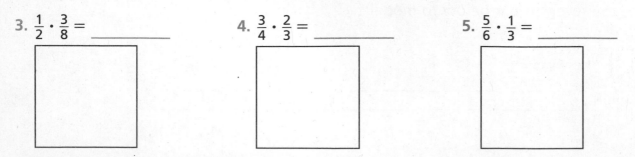

▶ Practice Multiplying Fractions

Find the product. You do not need to simplify your answer.

6. $\frac{1}{7} \cdot 6 =$ _____

7. $5 \cdot \frac{1}{4} =$ _____

8. $\frac{2}{3} \cdot 9 =$ _____

9. $4 \cdot \frac{3}{8} =$ _____

10. $\frac{1}{9} \cdot \frac{1}{2} =$ _____

11. $\frac{1}{3} \cdot \frac{1}{4} =$ _____

12. $\frac{2}{5} \cdot \frac{1}{3} =$ _____

13. $\frac{5}{6} \cdot \frac{3}{4} =$ _____

14. $\frac{3}{7} \cdot \frac{1}{3} =$ _____

15. $\frac{7}{10} \cdot \frac{7}{10} =$ _____

16. $\frac{3}{4} \cdot \frac{6}{11} =$ _____

17. $\frac{7}{8} \cdot \frac{8}{9} =$ _____

18. $\frac{4}{5} \cdot \frac{4}{5} =$ _____

19. $\frac{2}{7} \cdot \frac{4}{9} =$ _____

20. $\frac{4}{7} \cdot \frac{2}{9} =$ _____

21. $\frac{3}{4} \cdot 20 =$ _____

22. $\frac{1}{10} \cdot \frac{1}{10} =$ _____

23. $6 \cdot \frac{2}{3} =$ _____

24. $\frac{7}{8} \cdot \frac{1}{3} =$ _____

25. $\frac{7}{10} \cdot \frac{2}{7} =$ _____

26. $\frac{2}{5} \cdot 12 =$ _____

27. $\frac{1}{4} \cdot \frac{1}{2} =$ _____

28. $\frac{1}{5} \cdot 5 =$ _____

29. $\frac{6}{7} \cdot \frac{7}{8} =$ _____

▶ Fraction Word Problems

Represent the problem with an equation. Then solve.

Show your work.

30. Of the 304 people who attended the school play, $\frac{5}{8}$ were students. How many of the people who attended were students?

_____

31. One lap around the track is $\frac{1}{4}$ mile. Abby ran around the track 13 times. How far did she run?

_____

32. Cam is filling his bathtub. The tub holds 32 gallons of water. It is now $\frac{4}{7}$ full. How many gallons of water are in the tub?

_____

33. One third of the campers at a summer camp signed up for an arts-and-crafts class. Of these campers, one fifth signed up for woodworking. What fraction of the campers signed up for woodworking?

_____

34. Two thirds of the students in the orchestra play string instruments. Half of the students who play string instruments play violins. What fraction of all the students in the orchestra play violins?

_____

35. Ms. Hernandez knitted a scarf for her grandson. The scarf is $\frac{5}{6}$ yard long and $\frac{2}{9}$ yard wide. What is the area of the scarf?

_____

Multiply a Fraction by a Fraction

CA CC Content Standards 5.NF.4, 5.NF.4a, 5.NF.6
Mathematical Practices MP.1, MP.3, MP.6

▶ Simplify and Multiply Fractions

Multiply. Simplify first if you can.

1. $\frac{2}{3} \cdot 30 =$ _____

2. $\frac{2}{5} \cdot 35 =$ _____

3. $\frac{5}{6} \cdot 4 =$ _____

4. $\frac{7}{16} \cdot 8 =$ _____

5. $\frac{7}{20} \cdot \frac{5}{14} =$ _____

6. $\frac{2}{16} \cdot \frac{4}{21} =$ _____

7. $\frac{9}{10} \cdot \frac{7}{10} =$ _____

8. $\frac{7}{15} \cdot \frac{10}{21} =$ _____

9. $\frac{5}{24} \cdot \frac{6}{25} =$ _____

10. $\frac{5}{8} \cdot \frac{32}{45} =$ _____

11. $\frac{8}{49} \cdot \frac{7}{10} =$ _____

12. $\frac{7}{25} \cdot \frac{3}{4} =$ _____

13. Which fraction is not equivalent to the others?

$\frac{3}{9}$ $\frac{1}{3}$ $\frac{8}{24}$ $\frac{10}{30}$ $\frac{6}{18}$ $\frac{9}{36}$ $\frac{20}{60}$

▶ Solve Word Problems

Write an equation. Then solve.

Show your work.

14. In the Fireside Ski Shop, $\frac{11}{28}$ of the ski caps have tassels. Of the caps with tassels, $\frac{7}{11}$ are blue. What fraction of the caps in the shop are blue with tassels?

_____

15. In the shop, $\frac{27}{32}$ of the jackets have zippers. Of the jackets with zippers, $\frac{8}{9}$ have hoods. What fraction of the jackets in the shop have both zippers and hoods?

_____

16. Five of the 16 workers in the shop know how to ski. $\frac{1}{5}$ of those who can ski know how to snowboard. What fraction of the workers can ski and snowboard?

▶ What's the Error?

Dear Math Students,

I multiplied $\frac{7}{12} \cdot \frac{3}{4}$, but I think my answer is wrong. When you take a fraction of a fraction, you should get a smaller fraction. But my answer is larger. What mistake did I make? How do I correct it?

$$\frac{7}{\overset{12}{\underset{3}{\cancel{12}}}} \cdot \frac{3}{\underset{1}{\cancel{4}}} = \frac{21}{3} = 7$$

Your friend,
Puzzled Penguin

17. Write a response to Puzzled Penguin.

_____

_____

_____

_____

▶ Write Word Problems

Write a word problem that can be represented by the multiplication. Give the solution to your problem.

18. $\frac{3}{4} \cdot 8 = x$

_____

_____

_____

19. $\frac{8}{15} \cdot \frac{5}{12} = x$

_____

_____

_____

Multiplication Strategies

CA CC Content Standards **5.NF.4, 5.NF.4a, 5.NF.4b, 5.NF.5, 5.NF.5a, 5.NF.5b, 5.NF.6** Mathematical Practices **MP.1, MP.2, MP.7**

► Area Model for Mixed-Number Multiplication

A farmer has a rectangular field $1\frac{2}{3}$ miles long and $\frac{3}{4}$ mile wide. What is the area of the field?

Melinda knows the area is $1\frac{2}{3} \cdot \frac{3}{4}$. She explains how she makes an area model to find this product:

I need to make a rectangle with side lengths $1\frac{2}{3}$ units and $\frac{3}{4}$ unit. I start with 2 unit squares because one side of my rectangle will have a length greater than 1 unit.

I shade $\frac{3}{4}$ vertically in red. Horizontally, I shade 1 square and $\frac{2}{3}$ of another in blue. The overlap has an area of $1\frac{2}{3} \cdot \frac{3}{4}$, but I can't tell what this area is.

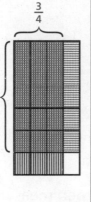

I divide the top square horizontally into thirds too. So, $\frac{5}{3}$ is shaded horizontally. Now, I can see that each unit square is divided into twelfths.

There are 15 twelfths in the overlap, so $1\frac{2}{3} \cdot \frac{3}{4} = \frac{15}{12}$, which is $1\frac{1}{4}$. The area of the field is $1\frac{1}{4}$ miles.

When I rewrite the factor $1\frac{2}{3}$ as a fraction, I can see that the product is the product of the numerators over the product of the denominators.

$$1\frac{2}{3} \cdot \frac{3}{4} = \frac{5}{3} \cdot \frac{3}{4} = \frac{15}{12} = \frac{5}{4} = 1\frac{1}{4}$$

Discuss this model for $1\frac{2}{5} \cdot 1\frac{1}{2}$ with your partner. Then answer the questions.

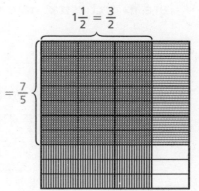

1. What unit fraction does each of the smallest rectangles represent?

   _____

2. How many unit-fraction rectangles are in the overlap?

   _____

3. Express the product of $1\frac{2}{5} \cdot 1\frac{1}{2}$ as a fraction and as a mixed number.

   _____

4. Rewrite $1\frac{2}{5} \cdot 1\frac{1}{2}$ as a product of fractions. Is the product equal to the product of the numerators over the product of the denominators?

   _____

► Practice Multiplying Mixed Numbers

Find each product by first rewriting each mixed number as a fraction.

5. $\frac{5}{6} \cdot 1\frac{1}{3} =$ _____

6. $3\frac{2}{3} \cdot 7 =$ _____

7. $1\frac{3}{4} \cdot 2\frac{1}{4} =$ _____

8. $4\frac{1}{2} \cdot \frac{4}{5} =$ _____

9. $\frac{7}{8} \cdot 1\frac{2}{5} =$ _____

10. $5 \cdot 1\frac{7}{10} =$ _____

11. $1\frac{2}{3} \cdot 1\frac{2}{3} =$ _____

12. $\frac{1}{12} \cdot 2\frac{2}{9} =$ _____

► Solve Word Problems

**Represent the problem with an equation. Then solve.
Draw a diagram if you need to.**

13. Sara built a pen for her pet rabbits. The pen measures $2\frac{5}{6}$ yards by $1\frac{1}{2}$ yards. What is the area of the pen?

_____

14. At Southtown High School, the number of students in band is $1\frac{3}{4}$ times the number in orchestra. If 56 students are in orchestra, how many are in band?

_____

15. A bucket holds $2\frac{3}{4}$ gallons of water. The bucket is $\frac{5}{8}$ full. How much water is in the bucket?

_____

16. Jacob's favorite movie is $1\frac{5}{6}$ hours long. He says he has watched the movie $5\frac{1}{2}$ times. If that is true, how many hours has Jacob spent watching the movie?

_____

CA CC Content Standards 5.NF.1, 5.NF.2, 5.NF.4, 5.NF.4a, 5.NF.5, 5.NF.5a, 5.NF.5b, 5.NF.6 Mathematical Practices MP.1, MP.2, MP.3, MP.6, MP.8

► Compare Multiplication and Addition

These fraction bars show how we add and multiply fractions.

Add $\frac{2}{5} + \frac{3}{5} = \frac{5}{5}$

Take $\frac{2}{5}$ of the whole

Multiply $\frac{3}{5} \cdot \frac{2}{5} = \frac{6}{25}$

Then take $\frac{3}{5}$ of each fifth.

1. Which problem above has the greater answer?

_____

2. Circle the problem that will have the greater answer. Then solve.

$\frac{2}{7} + \frac{3}{7} =$ _____ $\frac{3}{7} \cdot \frac{2}{7} =$ _____

3. The fractions in the problems at the right have different denominators. problem Circle the that will have the greater answer. Then solve.

$\frac{1}{6} + \frac{3}{4} =$ _____ $\frac{3}{4} \cdot \frac{1}{6} =$ _____

► Compare Fraction and Whole-Number Operations

Tell whether the answer will be less than or greater than the red number.

4. $a + b$ 5. $a - b$ 6. $b \cdot a$

7. $\frac{a}{b} + \frac{c}{d}$ 8. $\frac{a}{b} - \frac{c}{d}$ 9. $\frac{c}{d} \cdot \frac{a}{b}$

10. How is multiplying fractions different from multiplying whole numbers?

_____

_____

Keep in Mind
a and b are whole numbers greater than 1.
All of the fractions are less than 1.

► Comparison Problems with Mixed Operations

Amber, a very fit snail, moved $\frac{7}{9}$ yard in an hour. She challenged the other snails to try to do better.

Write how far each snail went.

11. Willy moved $\frac{4}{5}$ as far as Amber. _____

12. Dusty went $\frac{1}{3}$ yard less than Amber. _____

13. Pearl went twice as far as Amber. _____

14. Casey moved $\frac{4}{9}$ yard more than Amber. _____

15. Minnie moved half as far as Amber. _____

16. Make up your own question about another snail, Shelly. Ask a classmate to solve it.

_____

_____

_____

► Properties and Fractions

Commutative Property of Multiplication

$$\frac{a}{b} \cdot \frac{c}{d} = \frac{c}{d} \cdot \frac{a}{b}$$

Look at the proof of the **Commutative Property** below.

$$\frac{a}{b} \cdot \frac{c}{d} \quad = \quad \frac{a \cdot c}{b \cdot d} \quad = \quad \frac{c \cdot a}{d \cdot b} \quad = \quad \frac{c}{d} \cdot \frac{a}{b}$$

Step 1   Step 2   Step 3

17. Explain why each step is true.

Step 1 _____

Step 2 _____

Step 3 _____

Relate Fraction Operations

© Houghton Mifflin Harcourt Publishing Company

▶ Properties and Fractions (continued)

Associative Property of Multiplication

$$\frac{a}{b} \cdot \left(\frac{c}{d} \cdot \frac{e}{f}\right) = \left(\frac{a}{b} \cdot \frac{c}{d}\right) \cdot \frac{e}{f}$$

Look at the proof of the **Associative Property** below.

$$\frac{a}{b} \cdot \left(\frac{c}{d} \cdot \frac{e}{f}\right) = \frac{a}{b} \cdot \frac{c \cdot e}{d \cdot f} = \frac{a \cdot (c \cdot e)}{b \cdot (d \cdot f)} = \frac{(a \cdot c) \cdot e}{(b \cdot d) \cdot f} = \frac{a \cdot c}{b \cdot d} \cdot \frac{e}{f} = \left(\frac{a}{b} \cdot \frac{c}{d}\right) \cdot \frac{e}{f}$$

$\quad\quad\quad\quad\quad$ Step 1 $\quad\quad$ Step 2 $\quad\quad$ Step 3 $\quad\quad$ Step 4 $\quad\quad$ Step 5

18. Explain why each step is true.

Step 1 _____

Step 2 _____

Step 3 _____

Step 4 _____

Step 5 _____

Distributive Property

$$\frac{a}{b} \cdot \left(\frac{c}{d} + \frac{e}{f}\right) = \frac{a}{b} \cdot \frac{c}{d} + \frac{a}{b} \cdot \frac{e}{f}$$

For example, the **Distributive Property** tells us that

$$\frac{1}{2} \cdot \left(\frac{2}{3} + \frac{1}{4}\right) = \frac{1}{2} \cdot \frac{2}{3} + \frac{1}{2} \cdot \frac{1}{4}$$

19. Find the value of $\frac{1}{2} \cdot \left(\frac{2}{3} + \frac{1}{4}\right)$ by adding inside the parentheses first and then multiplying.

_____

20. Find the value of $\frac{1}{2} \cdot \frac{2}{3} + \frac{1}{2} \cdot \frac{1}{4}$ by multiplying and then adding.

_____

21. How do your answers to Exercises 19 and 20 compare?

_____

_____

▶ Mixed Practice

Find the value of the expression.

22. $\frac{4}{5} \cdot \frac{3}{7}$ _____

23. $\frac{4}{5} - \frac{3}{7}$ _____

24. $6 \cdot 1\frac{1}{3}$ _____

25. $6 + 1\frac{1}{3}$ _____

26. $1\frac{1}{2} + \frac{2}{3}$ _____

27. $1\frac{1}{2} \cdot \frac{2}{3}$ _____

28. $\frac{5}{8} \cdot \frac{8}{5}$ _____

29. $\frac{5}{8} + \frac{8}{5}$ _____

Write an equation. Then solve.

30. Daniel puts some wheat flour into an empty bowl. Then he adds $\frac{2}{3}$ cup rye flour to make a total of $2\frac{5}{12}$ cups of flour. How much wheat flour is in the bowl?

_____

31. Mañuela has a bag containing $5\frac{1}{3}$ cups of sugar. She uses $\frac{1}{8}$ of the sugar in a recipe. How much sugar does she use?

_____

32. Ashanti has a bag that contains $4\frac{1}{4}$ cups of rice. She uses $\frac{2}{3}$ cup. How much rice is left in the bag?

_____

33. Seth's route to school is $1\frac{3}{10}$ miles long. He has walked $\frac{4}{5}$ mile so far. How much farther does he have to go?

_____

34. Mara's walk to school is $1\frac{2}{5}$ miles. She is $\frac{5}{8}$ of the way there. How far has she walked so far?

_____

Relate Fraction Operations

Name _____ Date _____

CA CC Content Standards 5.NF.1, 5.NF.2, 5.NF.4, 5.NF.5a, 5.NF.6 Mathematical Practices MP.1, MP.2, MP.3, MP.6

▶ Add, Subtract, Compare, and Multiply

The fraction box to the right shows the same two fractions compared, added, subtracted, and multiplied.

	$\frac{1}{3}$ and $\frac{1}{6}$
>	$\frac{1}{3} > \frac{1}{6}$ or $\frac{2}{6} > \frac{1}{6}$
+	$\frac{1}{3} + \frac{1}{6} = \frac{2}{6} + \frac{1}{6} = \frac{3}{6} = \frac{1}{2}$
−	$\frac{1}{3} - \frac{1}{6} = \frac{2}{6} - \frac{1}{6} = \frac{1}{6}$
·	$\frac{1}{3} \cdot \frac{1}{6} = \frac{1}{18}$

Complete the fraction box.

1.

	$\frac{2}{5}$ and $\frac{7}{10}$
>	
+	
−	
·	

2.

	$\frac{3}{5}$ and $\frac{4}{7}$
>	
+	
−	
·	

▶ What's the Error?

Dear Math Students,

One of my friends said that he would give $\frac{1}{2}$ of his sandwich to me and $\frac{1}{2}$ of his sandwich to my sister. My sister said, "But then you won't have any left for yourself." This doesn't make sense to me. I know that $\frac{1}{2} + \frac{1}{2} = \frac{2}{4}$. My friend should have plenty left for himself. Did I do something wrong? What do you think?

Puzzled Penguin

3. Write a response to Puzzled Penguin.

_____

_____

_____

▶ Word Problems with Mixed Operations

Solve.   *Show your work.*

4. Yesterday Mr. Swenson made $2\frac{3}{4}$ quarts of strawberry jam and $1\frac{1}{8}$ quarts of raspberry jam. How much more strawberry jam did he make than raspberry?

   _____

5. Today Mr. Swenson is making $\frac{2}{5}$ quart of grape jelly. He will give $\frac{1}{2}$ of this amount to his neighbor. How much jelly will the neighbor get?

   _____

6. Mr. Swenson is also making $2\frac{1}{6}$ quarts of cherry jelly and $3\frac{1}{12}$ quarts of orange jelly. He will mix the two kinds together. How much of this mixed jelly will he have?

   _____

7. Yesterday Mr. Swenson made $\frac{7}{10}$ quart of blueberry jam. His family ate $\frac{1}{10}$ of it. How much of the blueberry jam is left?

   _____

8. Suppose Mr. Swenson has jars that hold $\frac{5}{6}$ quart, jars that hold $\frac{3}{4}$ quart, and jars that hold $\frac{2}{3}$ quart. Which size holds the most? Which size holds the least? How do you know?

   _____

9. Mr. Swenson made $6\frac{2}{3}$ quarts of jam last weekend. This weekend he plans to make $1\frac{1}{2}$ times this much. How much jam will he make this weekend?

   _____

▶ Predict and Multiply

Predict whether the product will be greater than, less than, or equal to the second factor. Then compute the product.

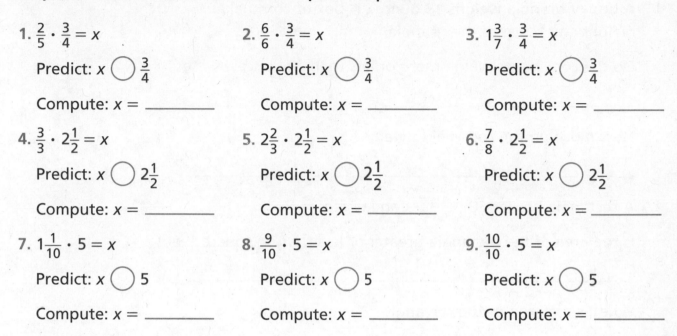

1. $\frac{2}{5} \cdot \frac{3}{4} = x$

   Predict: $x \bigcirc \frac{3}{4}$

   Compute: $x =$ _____

2. $\frac{6}{6} \cdot \frac{3}{4} = x$

   Predict: $x \bigcirc \frac{3}{4}$

   Compute: $x =$ _____

3. $1\frac{3}{7} \cdot \frac{3}{4} = x$

   Predict: $x \bigcirc \frac{3}{4}$

   Compute: $x =$ _____

4. $\frac{3}{3} \cdot 2\frac{1}{2} = x$

   Predict: $x \bigcirc 2\frac{1}{2}$

   Compute: $x =$ _____

5. $2\frac{2}{3} \cdot 2\frac{1}{2} = x$

   Predict: $x \bigcirc 2\frac{1}{2}$

   Compute: $x =$ _____

6. $\frac{7}{8} \cdot 2\frac{1}{2} = x$

   Predict: $x \bigcirc 2\frac{1}{2}$

   Compute: $x =$ _____

7. $1\frac{1}{10} \cdot 5 = x$

   Predict: $x \bigcirc 5$

   Compute: $x =$ _____

8. $\frac{9}{10} \cdot 5 = x$

   Predict: $x \bigcirc 5$

   Compute: $x =$ _____

9. $\frac{10}{10} \cdot 5 = x$

   Predict: $x \bigcirc 5$

   Compute: $x =$ _____

▶ Generalize

Complete the statement with *greater than*, *less than*, or *equal to*.

10. Multiplying any number, *n*, by a factor less than 1 gives a product _____ *n*.

11. Multiplying any number, *n*, by a factor equal to 1 gives a product _____ *n*.

12. Multiplying any number, *n*, by a factor greater than 1 gives a product _____ *n*.

Multiplying a fraction by a fraction equal to 1 gives an equivalent fraction. It is the same as multiplying both the numerator and denominator by the same number.

$$\frac{4}{7} = \frac{4}{7} \cdot \frac{3}{3} = \frac{12}{21} \qquad \frac{4}{7} = \frac{4 \cdot 3}{7 \cdot 3} = \frac{12}{21}$$

Multiply the fraction by a factor equal to 1 to create an equivalent fraction.

13. $\frac{4}{5}$

14. $\frac{3}{11}$

15. $\frac{5}{8}$

▶ Predict and Solve

Solve.   *Show your work.*

16. A box of granola weighs 18 ounces. A box of corn flakes weighs $\frac{7}{9}$ as much as the granola.

    Do the corn flakes weigh more or less than 18 ounces?

    _____

    How much do the corn flakes weigh?

    _____

17. A rectangle has length $3\frac{1}{4}$ feet and width $1\frac{1}{3}$ feet.

    Is the area of the rectangle greater or less than $3\frac{1}{4}$ square feet?

    _____

    What is the area of the rectangle?

    _____

18. The number of students on the football team is $1\frac{3}{4}$ times the number on the basketball team. There are 16 students on the basketball team.

    Are there more or fewer than 16 students on the football team?

    _____

    How many students are on the football team?

    _____

19. It's $9\frac{4}{5}$ miles from Justin's house to the art museum. The distance to the history museum is $\frac{9}{10}$ this far.

    Is the history museum more or less than $9\frac{4}{5}$ miles from Justin's house?

    _____

    How far from Justin's house is the history museum?

    _____

Name _____   **Date** _____

CA CC Content Standards 5.NF.3, 5.NF.4, 5.NF.4a, 5.NF.7, 5.NF.7a, 5.NF.7b Mathematical Practices MP.1, MP.3, MP.4, MP.6, MP.8

► Explore Fractional Shares

There are 4 people in the Walton family, but there are only 3 waffles. How can the Waltons share the waffles equally?

Divide each waffle into 4 pieces.

Each person's share of one waffle is $\frac{1}{4}$.
Since there are 3 waffles, each person gets 3 of the $\frac{1}{4}$s, or $\frac{3}{4}$ of a whole waffle.

$$3 \div 4 = 3 \cdot \frac{1}{4} = \frac{3}{4}$$

1. Suppose there are 5 people and 4 waffles.

   What is each person's share of 1 waffle? _____

   What is each person's share of 4 waffles? _____

   Complete the equation: $4 \div 5 =$ _____ $\cdot$ _____ $=$ _____

2. Suppose there are 10 people and 7 waffles.

   What is each person's share of 1 waffle? _____

   What is each person's share of 7 waffles? _____

   Complete the equation: $7 \div 10 =$ _____ $\cdot$ _____ $=$ _____

Complete.

3. $5 \div 6 =$ _____ $\cdot$ _____ $=$ _____

4. $4 \div 9 =$ _____ $\cdot$ _____ $=$ _____

Give your answer in the form of an equation.

5. How can you divide 7 waffles equally among 8 people?

   _____

6. How can you divide 39 waffles equally among 5 serving plates?

   _____

7. Discuss why this equation is true for any whole numbers n and d, except $d = 0$.

   $$n \div d = n \cdot \frac{1}{d} = \frac{n}{d}$$

   n unit fractions $\frac{1}{d}$

▶ Divide by a Unit Fraction

8. How many $\frac{1}{8}$s are there in 1? Write a division equation to show this.

_____

one whole

9. How many $\frac{1}{8}$s are there in 3? Write a division equation to show this.

_____

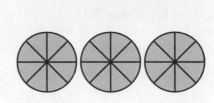

10. Why can you also use the multiplication equation 3 · 8 = 24 to show how many $\frac{1}{8}$s are in 3?

_____

_____

11. How many $\frac{1}{4}$s are there in 5? Write a division and a multiplication equation to show this.

_____

12. Complete the equation. w and d are whole numbers and d is not 0. $w \div \frac{1}{d} =$ _____

Write a division equation. Then solve.

Show your work.

13. Olivia made 9 sandwiches and cut each one into fourths. How many fourths does she have?

_____

14. The 10 members of a hiking club will walk 9 miles. Each person will carry the food pack for an equal distance. How far will each hiker carry the food pack?

_____

15. Damon has a 6-pound bag of cat food. He feeds his cat $\frac{1}{8}$ pound every day. How many days will the bag last?

_____

16. Jodie and 7 friends share 12 oranges equally. How many oranges does each person get? Give your answer as a mixed number.

When Dividing Is Also Multiplying

▶ Unit Fractions in Action

Karen's 5 grandchildren came to visit for 3 days. Karen found a long roll of drawing paper. She said, "I'll cut this paper into 3 equal parts, and we'll use one part on each day." Then she cut the first part into 5 equal parts so each grandchild could make a drawing. She asked her grandchildren, "What part of the whole roll of paper do each of you have? What math problem is this? Make a drawing so Sammy will understand."

Tommy, the oldest, said, "Today we are using $\frac{1}{3}$ of the whole roll because we have 3 equal parts."

Lucy said, "Then we cut that $\frac{1}{3}$ into 5 equal parts. So we found $\frac{1}{3} \div 5$, a unit fraction divided by the whole number 5."

Asha said, "But we have to divide each of the other two thirds into 5 equal parts to find out how many equal parts we have in all. That's like multiplying by $\frac{1}{5}$!"

Phoebe said, "Oh look, we have 15 equal parts in all. So today we are each using $\frac{1}{15}$ of the whole roll."

Sammy, the youngest grandchild said, "So dividing by 5 is the same as multiplying by $\frac{1}{5}$ because that also means finding one of five equal parts."

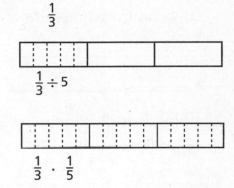

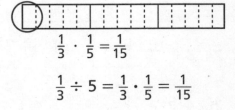

$$\frac{1}{3} \div 5 = \frac{1}{3} \cdot \frac{1}{5} = \frac{1}{15}$$

The children said, "So dividing by a whole number w is the same as multiplying by $\frac{1}{w}$."

$$\frac{1}{d} \div w = \frac{1}{d} \cdot \frac{1}{w} = \frac{1}{d \cdot w}$$

Solve.

17. $\frac{1}{2} \div 3 = \frac{1}{2} \cdot$ _____ = _____

18. $\frac{1}{5} \div 2 = \frac{1}{5} \cdot$ _____ = _____

19. $\frac{1}{3} \div 4 = \frac{1}{3} \cdot$ _____ = _____

20. $\frac{1}{6} \div 4 = \frac{1}{6} \cdot$ _____ = _____

▶ Practice Division

$$n \div d = n \cdot \frac{1}{d} = \frac{n}{d} \qquad w \div \frac{1}{d} = w \cdot d \qquad \frac{1}{d} \div w = \frac{1}{d} \cdot \frac{1}{w} = \frac{1}{d \cdot w}$$

21. Describe patterns you see in the equations above.

_____

_____

_____

22. Why is dividing by a whole number the same as multiplying by a unit fraction with that number as its denominator?

_____

_____

23. Why does dividing w by a unit fraction $\frac{1}{d}$ make $w \cdot d$, a number greater than w?

_____

_____

24. $3 \div 10 = $ ___ $\cdot$ ___ $=$ ___

25. $5 \div 8 = $ ___ $\cdot$ ___ $=$ ___

26. $4 \div \frac{1}{3} = $ ___ $\cdot$ ___ $=$ ___

27. $7 \div \frac{1}{2} = $ ___ $\cdot$ ___ $=$ ___

28. $\frac{1}{2} \div 5 = $ ___ $\cdot$ ___ $=$ ___

29. $\frac{1}{3} \div 4 = $ ___ $\cdot$ ___ $=$ ___

30. For the two problems below, which answer will be greater? Explain.

$$\frac{1}{3} \div 5 \qquad\qquad 5 \div \frac{1}{3}$$

_____

_____

_____

3-11

Class Activity

Name _____ Date _____

CA CC Content Standards 5.NF.3, 5.NF.7, 5.NF.7a, 5.NF.7b, 5.NF.7c Mathematical Practices MP.1, MP.2, MP.4, MP.5, MP.6

▶ Division Situations and Diagrams

1. Consider the division problem $2 \div 5$.

Describe a situation this division could represent.

_____

_____

Draw a diagram to represent the division. Then find the solution.

2. Consider the division problem $4 \div \frac{1}{3}$.

Describe a situation this division could represent.

_____

_____

Draw a diagram to represent the division. Then find the solution.

3. Consider the division problem $\frac{1}{4} \div 2$.

Describe a situation this division could represent.

_____

_____

Draw a diagram to represent the division. Then find the solution.

© Houghton Mifflin Harcourt Publishing Company

UNIT 3 LESSON 11

Solve Division Problems **95**

► Division Word Problems

Write an equation. Then solve.

Show your work.

4. One lap around the track is $\frac{1}{4}$ mile. José wants to run 5 miles. How many times must he run around the track?

_____

5. There is $\frac{1}{6}$ of an extra large pizza left over in the fridge. If three friends share the pizza equally, what fraction of a whole pizza will each friend get?

_____

6. Oscar's aunt lives 50 miles away. This is 6 times as far as Oscar's grandfather lives. How far away does Oscar's grandfather live?

_____

7. A banner has a length of 10 feet and an area of 7 square feet. What is the width of the banner?

_____

8. Brady has three goldfish. This is $\frac{1}{5}$ times as many as Sam has. How many goldfish does Sam have?

_____

9. Lucy has $\frac{1}{2}$ hour to decorate a dozen cupcakes for a bake sale. How much time can she spend on each cupcake?

_____

10. If $\frac{1}{8}$ pound of uncooked rice makes one serving, how many servings are in a 15-pound bag of rice?

_____

11. On Wednesday, 72 people watched the softball game. It rained on Friday, so only 18 people watched the game. The number of people who watched on Friday is how many times the number who watched on Wednesday?

_____

Solve Division Problems

CA CC Content Standards 5.NF.4, 5.NF.6, 5.NF.7, 5.NF.7a, 5.NF.7b, 5.NF.7c Mathematical Practices MP.1, MP.2, MP.3, MP.6, MP.8

▶ Solve Word Problems with Multiplication and Division

Decide whether you need to multiply or divide. Then solve.   *Show your work.*

1. A turtle crawls 3 yards in an hour. How far will it crawl in 2 hours?

   _____

   How far will the turtle crawl in $\frac{1}{4}$ hour?

   _____

2. Emily has 2 tons of sand. She will move it by wheelbarrow to the garden. Her wheelbarrow holds $\frac{1}{10}$ ton. How many trips will she make?

   _____

3. Tawana has 3 pounds of nuts. She is using them to fill small bags with $\frac{1}{4}$ pound each. How many bags can she fill?

   _____

4. Roberto has a recipe that calls for 4 cups of flour. He wants to use only $\frac{1}{2}$ of the recipe today. How much flour will he need?

   _____

5. A picnic jug holds 1 gallon of lemonade. Each paper cup holds $\frac{1}{12}$ gallon. How many paper cups can be filled?

   _____

6. It rained on $\frac{2}{5}$ of all the days last month. On $\frac{1}{6}$ of these rainy days, there were thunderstorms. On what fraction of the days last month were there thunderstorms?

   _____

▶ Generalize Results

In the equations below, a and b are whole numbers greater than 1. $\frac{n}{d}$ is a fraction less than 1. $\frac{1}{d}$ is a unit fraction. Answer the questions about the equations.

Parts of a Division Problem

$$4 \div \frac{1}{3} = 12$$

dividend   divisor   quotient

Multiplication

7. $a \cdot b = c$

   Will c be greater than or less than a? _____ Why?

   _____

   _____

8. $a \cdot \frac{n}{d} = c$

   Will c be greater than or less than a? _____ Why?

   _____

   _____

Division

9. $a \div b = c$

   Will c be greater than or less than a? _____ Why?

   _____

   _____

10. $a \div \frac{1}{d} = c$

    Will c be greater than or less than a? _____ Why?

    _____

    _____

Circle the problem with the greater answer.
Do not try to calculate the answer.

11. $4{,}826 \cdot 581$ $4{,}826 \div 581$

12. $347 \cdot \frac{1}{72}$ $347 \div \frac{1}{72}$

Distinguish Multiplication from Division

Name _____ **Date** _____

▶ Predict the Size of the Result

Decide what operation to use, predict the size of the result, then solve the problem.

Show your work.

13. Lucy spends 4 hours a week babysitting. Her sister Lily spends $\frac{7}{8}$ as much time babysitting. Does Lily babysit for more or less than 4 hours?

_____

Now find the exact amount of time Lily babysits.

_____

14. Yoshi has a rope 30 feet long. He must cut it into pieces that are each $\frac{1}{4}$-foot long. Will he get more or fewer than 30 pieces?

_____

Now find the exact number of pieces Yoshi will get.

_____

15. Carlos can throw a ball 14 yards. His friend Raul can throw $\frac{3}{7}$ of that distance. Is Raul's throw longer or shorter than 14 yards?

_____

Now find the exact length of Raul's throw.

_____

16. An apple orchard covers 12 acres. There is a watering spout for every $\frac{1}{4}$ acre. Are there more or fewer than 12 watering spouts?

_____

Now find the exact number of watering spouts in the orchard.

_____

Name _____   Date _____

▶ What's the Error?

Dear Math Students,

I have to divide 5 cups in half for a recipe. Here's what I did:

$$5 \div \frac{1}{2} = 5 \cdot \frac{2}{1} = 10$$

I know I did the division correctly, but my answer should be less than 5, not more. Can you explain my mistake and help me fix it?

Your friend,
Puzzled Penguin

17. Write a response to Puzzled Penguin.

_____

_____

_____

▶ Summarize Fraction Operations

18. You have just won a prize on a new quiz show called *Quick Thinking*. The prize will be *n* album downloads from an online music store. You have a chance to change your prize if you think you can make it better. The screen shows the choices you have. Which will you choose?

$$n \div \frac{1}{3}$$
$$n \cdot \frac{1}{3}$$

_____

19. Suppose $n = 6$. How many albums have you won? _____

20. Suppose $n = 12$. How many albums have you won? _____

21. Discuss what you have learned about the size of the answers when you mulitiply and divide by whole numbers and by fractions.

Distinguish Multiplication from Division

CA CC Content Standards 5.NF.1, 5.NF.2, 5.NF.3, 5.NF.4,
5.NF.5, 5.NF.5a, 5.NF.6, 5.NF.7, 5.NF.7a, 5.NF.7b, 5.NF.7c,
5.MD.2 Mathematical Practices MP.1

▶ Choose the Operation

Decide what operation to use. Then solve.

1. Hala can ride her bike $7\frac{1}{2}$ miles in an hour.
   How far will she ride in 3 hours? How far
   will she ride in $\frac{1}{3}$ of an hour?

   _____
   _____
   _____

2. Eryn's pet rabbit eats $\frac{1}{12}$ pound of
   food every day. If Eryn buys rabbit food in
   5-pound bags, how many days does one bag
   of rabbit food last?

   _____
   _____
   _____
   _____

3. Mr. Dayton uses 8 cups of flour to make
   three identical loaves of bread. How much
   flour is in each loaf?

   _____
   _____
   _____

4. Jonathan can throw a baseball $10\frac{1}{3}$ yards. His
   brother Joey can throw a baseball $13\frac{1}{12}$ yards.
   How much farther can Joey throw the ball?

   _____
   _____
   _____

5. Kim bought $\frac{3}{8}$ pound of sunflower seeds
   and $\frac{3}{16}$ pound of thistle seed for her bird
   feeder. How much seed did she buy in all?

   _____
   _____
   _____

6. Casandra's fish bowl holds $\frac{9}{10}$ gallon of
   water. It is now $\frac{2}{3}$ full. How much water
   is in the bowl?

   _____
   _____
   _____

▶ Predict and Solve

7. Marcus plays basketball for 9 hours each week.
   His friend Luis spends $\frac{5}{6}$ as much time playing
   basketball. Who plays more basketball?

   _____
   _____

   How much time does Luis spend playing
   basketball?

   _____

8. Stacey's long jump was 10 feet. That is $\frac{5}{6}$ foot
   longer than Ron's long jump. Did Ron jump
   more or less than 10 feet?

   _____
   _____

   How long was Ron's jump?

   _____

Name _____ Date _____

▶ Practice Fraction Operations

Write the answer in simplest form.

9. $7 \div \frac{1}{3} =$ _____

10. $1\frac{5}{12} + 2\frac{5}{8} =$ _____

11. $\frac{1}{8} + \frac{5}{6} =$ _____

12. $\frac{4}{9} \cdot 8 =$ _____

13. $\frac{4}{7} - \frac{1}{3} =$ _____

14. $9 \div 10 =$ _____

15. $2\frac{3}{5} - 2\frac{6}{35} =$ _____

16. $\frac{2}{5} \cdot 5\frac{1}{2} =$ _____

17. $\frac{1}{6} + \frac{2}{9} =$ _____

18. $3\frac{1}{3} - 1\frac{3}{4} =$ _____

19. $1\frac{7}{8} \cdot 3\frac{2}{5} =$ _____

20. $\frac{1}{9} \div 3 =$ _____

Solve.

21. Mr. Jones's students recorded the number of hours they slept last night to the nearest quarter hour. The results are shown on this line plot.

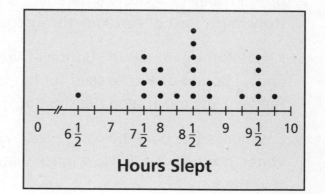

Hours Slept

a. What is the range of values for the data (the difference between the greatest value and the least value)?

_____

b. Six students slept $8\frac{1}{2}$ hours. What total number of hours do these six values represent?

_____

c. Olivia said, "The longest time value is $1\frac{1}{2}$ times the shortest time value." Is she correct? Explain.

_____

Review Operations with Fractions

Name _____   **Date** _____

CA CC Content Standards 5.NF.6, 5.NF.7c
Mathematical Practices MP.4, MP.5, MP.6, MP.7, MP8

▶ Math and Marching Bands

The musicians in a marching band play many different kinds of musical instruments. Each type of instrument represents a part of the whole, which is all of the instruments in the band.

The circle graph below shows the fraction of all of the instruments in a school marching band that are bass drums.

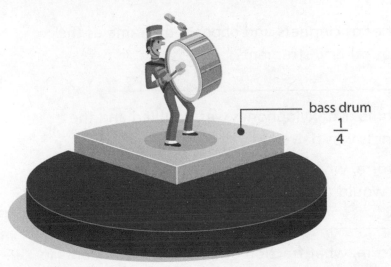

bass drum
$\frac{1}{4}$

Solve. Use the circle graph above.

Show your work.

1. The marching band has 15 bass drums. How many instruments altogether are in the band?

_____

► Math and Marching Bands (continued)

Solve. Use the circle graph.

2. How many instruments of each kind are in the band?

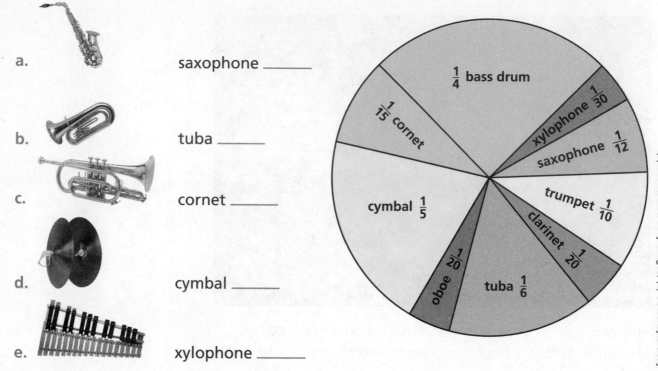

a.   saxophone _____

b.   tuba _____

c.   cornet _____

d.   cymbal _____

e.   xylophone _____

3. The total number of clarinets and oboes is the same as the number of what other instrument?

_____

4. Suppose the number of xylophones was doubled and the number of cornets was halved.

a. In simplest form, what fraction of all of the instruments in the band would the new number of xylophones represent?

_____

b. In simplest form, what fraction of all of the instruments in the band would the new number of cornets represent?

_____

c. In simplest form, what fraction represents all of the *other* instruments in the band?

_____

© Houghton Mifflin Harcourt Publishing Company • Image Credits: (t) ©Brand X Pictures/Alamy Images; (tc) ©Creatas/Getty Images; (c) ©PhotoDisc/Getty Images; (b) ©Stockbyte/Getty Images

Focus on Mathematical Practices

1. For numbers 1a–1d, without multiplying, use the symbols
   from the list on the right to indicate the product will compare
   with the factor. Symbols can be used more than once.

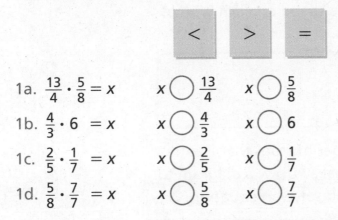

$$\boxed{<} \quad \boxed{>} \quad \boxed{=}$$

1a. $\frac{13}{4} \cdot \frac{5}{8} = x$ $x \bigcirc \frac{13}{4}$ $x \bigcirc \frac{5}{8}$

1b. $\frac{4}{3} \cdot 6 = x$ $x \bigcirc \frac{4}{3}$ $x \bigcirc 6$

1c. $\frac{2}{5} \cdot \frac{1}{7} = x$ $x \bigcirc \frac{2}{5}$ $x \bigcirc \frac{1}{7}$

1d. $\frac{5}{8} \cdot \frac{7}{7} = x$ $x \bigcirc \frac{5}{8}$ $x \bigcirc \frac{7}{7}$

2. Three packages of trail mix are shared equally between Alycia and
   her four classmates.

   Part A

   Each bar represents one package of trail mix. Shade the bars to
   show how much of each package of trail mix one person will get.

1 whole

1 whole

1 whole

   Part B

   How much of one package of trail mix will each person get?
   Write and solve an equation.

3. For the breakfast buffet, Mr. Walker must equally divide 12 loaves
   of bread between seven platters. How many loaves of bread are
   placed on each platter? Write and solve an equation.

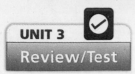
4. Elin has $\frac{1}{3}$ hour to warm up for her gymnastics meet. She must complete each of 6 different stretches. She spends an equal amount of time on each type of stretch and she does not take a break. How long, in hours, does she spend on each type of stretch? Write and solve an equation.

5. Ava has two frogs. This is $\frac{1}{3}$ the number of frogs that Heather has. How many frogs does Heather have? Draw a diagram to represent the division. Then write and solve an equation.

6. For a snack, Miss Johnson gives her class graham crackers. She has a package of 20 graham crackers to share equally among eight students. How many graham crackers should each student receive? Explain how you found your answer.

7. For numbers 7a–7d, select True or False for each the product.

7a. $\frac{3}{5} \cdot \frac{2}{7} = \frac{21}{10}$ ○ True   ○ False

7b. $\frac{2}{9} \cdot \frac{5}{3} = \frac{10}{27}$ ○ True   ○ False

7c. $\frac{7}{8} \cdot \frac{5}{9} = \frac{35}{72}$ ○ True   ○ False

7d. $\frac{1}{2} \cdot \frac{3}{5} = \frac{4}{10}$ ○ True   ○ False

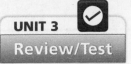

8. Juan needs to measure six cups of flour for a recipe. He only has a $\frac{1}{4}$ measuring cup. How many times must he fill the measuring cup to get six cups of flour?

For numbers 8a–8e, choose Yes or No to tell whether the equation can be used to solve the word problem shown above.

8a. $6 \cdot \frac{1}{4} = \bigcirc$ ○ Yes   ○ No

8b. $6 \cdot 4 = \bigcirc$ ○ Yes   ○ No

8c. $1 \cdot \frac{4}{6} = \bigcirc$ ○ Yes   ○ No

8d. $6 \div \frac{1}{4} = \bigcirc$ ○ Yes   ○ No

8e. $6 \div 4 = \bigcirc$ ○ Yes   ○ No

9. Ben has a piece of cord that is 40 feet long. He wants to cut the cord into pieces to tie up the tomato plants in his garden. How many pieces can he cut if each piece is $\frac{1}{2}$ foot long? Draw a diagram to represent the division. Then write and solve an equation to find the solution.

10. Of the fifth grade students, $\frac{15}{20}$ went to the book fair. Of the students who went to the book fair, $\frac{12}{16}$ bought at least one book. What fraction of fifth grade students bought at least one book? Show your work.

11. Marie plants flowers in a planter that is $1\frac{1}{2}$ feet long and $1\frac{2}{3}$ feet wide. She plans to cover the entire area with fertilizer. How much area will she need to spread with fertilizer?

_____ square feet

12. Of the coins in Simone's collection, $\frac{13}{25}$ are quarters. Of these quarters, $\frac{2}{3}$ are state quarters. What fraction of Simone's coins are state quarters?

13. A square *Do Not Enter* sign has a height and width of $2\frac{1}{2}$ feet.

Part A
Will the area of the sign be greater than or less than $2\frac{1}{2}$ square feet? Explain how you know.

Part B
What is the area of the sign? Show your work.

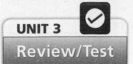

14. Patel drew the area model to help him solve a multiplication problem.

$\frac{4}{3}$ $\frac{5}{3}$

$\frac{3}{5}$ $\frac{3}{4}$

Part A

Use the numbers from the list on the right to complete the area model.

Part B

What is the answer to the problem Patel was working on? Show your work.

Without multiplying, choose the symbol from the box to compare the product on the left with the factor shown on the right.

15. $\frac{4}{5} \cdot \frac{3}{8}$ $\boxed{\begin{matrix} < \\ > \\ = \end{matrix}}$ $\frac{4}{5}$

16. $\frac{8}{6} \cdot \frac{2}{3}$ $\boxed{\begin{matrix} < \\ > \\ = \end{matrix}}$ $\frac{2}{3}$

17. $\frac{5}{5} \cdot \frac{3}{8}$ $\boxed{\begin{matrix} < \\ > \\ = \end{matrix}}$ $\frac{3}{8}$

18. Without multiplying, classify each product as being less than $\frac{2}{3}$, equal to $\frac{2}{3}$, or greater than $\frac{2}{3}$. Write the letter of each expression in the correct box.

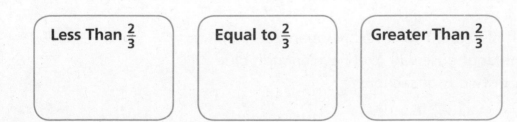

A $\frac{2}{3} \cdot \frac{1}{5}$ B $\frac{2}{3} \cdot \frac{8}{5}$ C $\frac{2}{3} \cdot \frac{9}{9}$ D $\frac{2}{3} \cdot \frac{6}{1}$ E $\frac{2}{3} \cdot \frac{8}{9}$ F $\frac{2}{3} \cdot 2$

Less Than $\frac{2}{3}$ Equal to $\frac{2}{3}$ Greater Than $\frac{2}{3}$

19. Hannah wants to divide five oranges equally among four children. She drew a model to find 5 ÷ 4. Is Hannah's model correct? Explain your reasoning using words, numbers, and pictures.

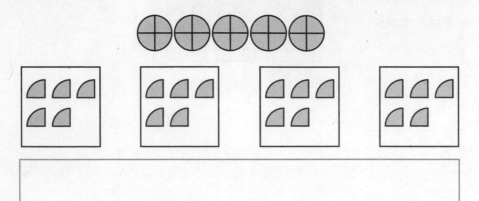

20. Axel paints his doghouse using leftover paint. He has two identical walls and two identical sections of roof unpainted. The dimensions of the rectangular wall and roof sections are listed in the table.

Part A

Complete the table by writing the area of one wall and one roof section.

Part	Length (ft)	Width (ft)	Total Area (ft²)
Wall	$1\frac{1}{3}$	$2\frac{1}{6}$	
Roof	$1\frac{1}{2}$	$2\frac{1}{12}$	

Part B

Axel has enough blue paint to cover six square feet. For which part of the doghouse will Axel have enough blue paint–two walls or two roof sections?

two _____

Dear Family,

Unit 4 of *Math Expressions* introduces students to multiplying with multidigit numbers using models and different recording methods. The main goal of this unit is to develop skills in multiplying with whole numbers and decimal numbers. Some additional goals are:

• to solve real world application problems;

• to understand patterns in the number of zeros in the product when multiplying a number by 10, 100, or 1,000;

• to use estimation to check the reasonableness of answers;

• to understand and use exponents to denote powers of 10.

Your child will learn and practice techniques such as Place Value Sections, Expanded Notation, and Shift Patterns to gain speed and accuracy in multidigit and decimal multiplication. Money examples will be used in multiplication with decimals.

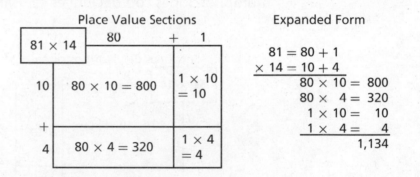

Throughout Unit 4, your child will solve real world problems that require multidigit multiplication as well as using rounding and mental math to estimate products.

If you have any questions, please call or write to me.

Sincerely,
Your child's teacher

 CA CC

Unit 4 addresses the following standards from the *Common Core State Standards for Mathematics with California Additions*: **5.NBT.1, 5.NBT.2, 5.NBT.3, 5.NBT.3b, 5.NBT.4, 5.NBT.5, 5.NBT.7,** and all Mathematical Practices.

Dear Family,

La Unidad 4 de *Math Expressions* introduce a los estudiantes a la multiplicación con números de varios dígitos por medio del uso de modelos y varios métodos de anotación. El objetivo principal de la unidad es desarrollar destrezas para multiplicar con números enteros y decimales. Algunos objetivos adicionales son:

• resolver problemas con aplicaciones a la vida diaria;

• reconocer patrones en el número de ceros en el producto al multiplicar un número por 10, 100 ó 1,000;

• usar la estimación para comprobar que las respuestas sean razonables;

• reconocer y usar exponentes para indicar potencias de 10.

Su niño aprenderá y practicará técnicas tales como Secciones de valor posicional, Notación extendida y Patrones de desplazamiento, para adquirir rapidez y exactitud en la multiplicación con números de varios dígitos y decimales. En las multiplicaciones con decimales se usarán ejemplos de dinero.

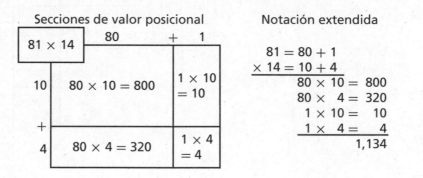

Secciones de valor posicional

81×14	80	+	1
10	$80 \times 10 = 800$		$1 \times 10 = 10$
+			
4	$80 \times 4 = 320$		$1 \times 4 = 4$

Notación extendida

$$81 = 80 + 1$$
$$\times\ 14 = 10 + 4$$
$$80 \times 10 = 800$$
$$80 \times\ 4 = 320$$
$$1 \times 10 =\ 10$$
$$1 \times\ 4 =\ 4$$
$$1,134$$

Durante el transcurso de la Unidad 4 su niño resolverá problemas de la vida diaria que requieran el uso de la multiplicación de números de varios dígitos, del redondeo, y del cálculo mental para estimar productos.

Si tiene alguna duda o algún comentario, por favor comuníquese conmigo.

Atentamente,
El maestro su niño

CA CC

En la Unidad 4 se aplican los siguientes estándares auxiliares, contenidos en los *Estándares estatales comunes de matemáticas con adiciones para california*: **5.NBT.1, 5.NBT.2, 5.NBT.3, 5.NBT.3b, 5.NBT.4, 5.NBT.5, 5.NBT.7** y todos los de prácticas matemáticas.

Name _____

Date _____

CA CC Content Standards 5.NBT.1, 5.NBT.2, 5.NBT.7
Mathematical Practices MP.1, MP.2, MP.4, MP.6, MP.8

VOCABULARY
shift

▶ Shifts with Whole Numbers

Jordan earns $243 a week. The money is shown at the right. Answer the questions about how much he will earn over time.

Jordan's Weekly Earnings

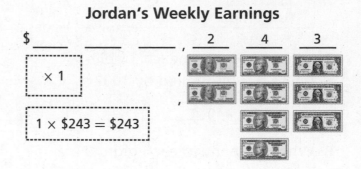

When you multiply by 10, the digits shift by one place to the left.

1. After 10 weeks, how much will Jordan have earned?

   _____

2. What happens to each $1-bill when it is multiplied by 10?

   _____

3. What happens to each other bill when it is multiplied by 10?

   _____

4. When you multiply by 10, does each digit **shift** to the right or left?

   _____

5. How many places does each digit shift?

   _____

After 10 Weeks

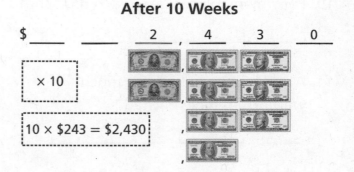

6. After 100 weeks, how much will Jordan have earned?

_____

7. What happens to each $1-bill when it is multiplied by 100?

_____

8. What happens to each digit when it is multiplied by 100?

_____

9. When you multiply by 100, does each digit shift to the right or left?

_____

10. How many places does each digit shift?

_____

11. After 1,000 weeks, how much will Jordan have earned?

_____

12. What happens to each $1-bill when it is multiplied by 1,000?

_____

13. What happens to each digit when it is multiplied by 1,000?

_____

14. When you multiply by 1,000, does each digit shift to the right or left?

_____

15. How many places does each digit shift?

_____

After 100 Weeks

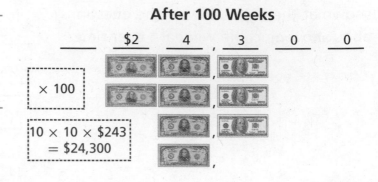

After 1,000 Weeks

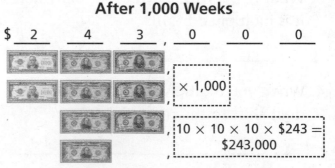

Name _____   Date _____

► See the Shift in Motion

Isabel earns $325 a week. Three students can show how the digits shift at the board when we multiply her earnings.

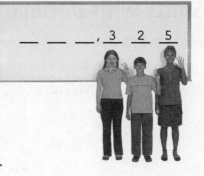

— — —, 3 2 5

Complete each exercise.

16. Suppose Isabel works for 10 weeks. Find her earnings.

___ ___ ___ , $3 2 5 [× 10 > ___ ___ $3 , 2 5 0 ___

$325 shifts _____ place(s) to the _____. It becomes 10 times as great.

17. Suppose Isabel works for 100 weeks. Find her earnings.

___ ___ ___ , $3 2 5 [× 100 > ___ $3 2 , 5 0 0 ___

$325 shifts _____ places to the _____. It becomes 100 times as great.

18. Suppose Isabel works for 1,000 weeks. Find her earnings.

___ ___ ___ , $3 2 5 [× 1,000 > $3 2 5 , 0 0 0 ___

$325 shifts _____ places to the _____. It becomes 1,000 times as great.

Complete each exercise.

19. $567 \times 10 =$ _____

20. $38 \times 1,000 =$ _____

21. $912 \times 100 =$ _____

22. $700 \times 10 =$ _____

23. The Skyway Express train travels about 800 miles a day. How far does it travel in 10 days?

_____

24. Since there are 30 days in April, about how far will the train travel during the month of April?

_____

▶ Shifts with Decimal Amounts

It costs $0.412 (41 and $\frac{2}{10}$ cents) for a factory to make a Red Phantom Marble. The money is shown here.

Cost of a Red Phantom Marble

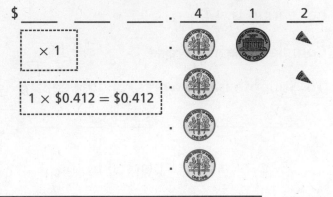

$ ____ ____ ____ . 4 1 2

× 1

1 × $0.412 = $0.412

Answer each question about the cost of making different numbers of Red Phantom Marbles.

25. How much does it cost to make 10 Red Phantom Marbles?

_____

26. What happens to each coin when it is multiplied by 10?

_____

27. What happens to each digit?

_____

28. When you multiply by 10, does each digit shift to the right or left?

_____

29. How many places does each digit shift?

_____

10 Red Phantom Marbles

$ ____ ____ 4 . 1 2 ____

× 10

10 × $0.412 = $4.12

30. How much does it cost to make 100 Red Phantom Marbles?

_____

31. What happens to each coin when you multiply by 100?

_____

32. What happens to each digit?

_____

33. When you multiply by 100, does each digit shift to the right or left?

_____

34. How many places does each digit shift?

_____

35. How much does it cost to make 1,000 Red Phantom Marbles?

_____

36. What happens to each coin when you multiply by 1,000?

_____

37. What happens to each digit?

_____

38. When you multiply by 1,000, does each digit shift to the right or left?

_____

39. How many places does each digit shift?

100 Red Phantom Marbles

$ _____ _4_ _1_ . _2_ _0_ _____

× 100

100 × $0.412 = $41.20

1,000 Red Phantom Marbles

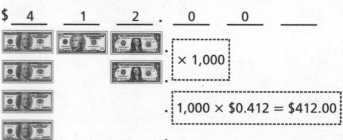

$ _4_ _1_ _2_ . _0_ _0_ _____

× 1,000

1,000 × $0.412 = $412.00

▶ Patterns in Multiplying with Zeros

Discuss patterns you see across each row and down each
column. Then state a generalization for multiplying numbers
with zeros.

×	3	30	300	3,000
2	a. $2 \times 3 = 6$	b. 2×30 $= 2 \times 3 \times 10$ $= 6 \times 10$ $= 60$	c. 2×300 $= 2 \times 3 \times 100$ $= 6 \times 100$ $= 600$	d. $2 \times 3,000$ $= 2 \times 3 \times 1,000$ $= 6 \times 1,000$ $= 6,000$
20	e. 20×3 $= 2 \times 10 \times 3$ $= 6 \times 10$ $= 60$	f. 20×30 $= 2 \times 10 \times 3$ $\times 10$ $= 6 \times 100$ $= 600$	g. 20×300 $= 2 \times 10 \times 3$ $\times 100$ $= 6 \times 1,000$ $= 6,000$	h. $20 \times 3,000$ $= 2 \times 10 \times 3$ $\times 1,000$ $= 6 \times 10,000$ $= 60,000$
200	i. 200×3 $= 2 \times 100 \times 3$ $= 6 \times 100$ $= 600$	j. 200×30 $= 2 \times 100 \times 3$ $\times 10$ $= 6 \times 1,000$ $= 6,000$	k. 200×300 $= 2 \times 100 \times 3$ $\times 100$ $= 6 \times 10,000$ $= 60,000$	l. $200 \times 3,000$ $= 2 \times 100 \times 3$ $\times 1,000$ $= 6 \times 100,000$ $= 600,000$
2,000	m. $2,000 \times 3$ $= 2 \times 1,000 \times 3$ $= 6 \times 1,000$ $= 6,000$	n. $2,000 \times 30$ $= 2 \times 1,000 \times 3$ $\times 10$ $= 6 \times 10,000$ $= 60,000$	o. $2,000 \times 300$ $= 2 \times 1,000 \times 3$ $\times 100$ $= 6 \times 100,000$ $= 600,000$	p. $2,000 \times 3,000$ $= 2 \times 1,000 \times 3$ $\times 1,000$ $= 6 \times 1,000,000$ $= 6,000,000$

Solve.

40.	41.	42.	43.	44.
60 × 3	60 × 30	600 × 30	600 × 300	6,000 × 30

© Houghton Mifflin Harcourt Publishing Company

VOCABULARY
base
exponent
exponential form
power of ten

▶ Powers of Ten

Expressions with repeated factors such as $10 \times 10 \times 10$ can be written by using a base with an exponent. The **base** is the number that is used as the repeated factor. The **exponent** is a number that tell how many times the base is used as a factor.

$$1{,}000 = \underbrace{10 \times 10 \times 10}_{\text{3 factors}} = 10^{\overset{\text{exponent}}{3}}$$

base

When you represent a number using a base and an exponent, you are using **exponential form**.

Exponential form: 10^3

Word form: ten raised to the third power or
the third **power of ten**

Write each expression as repeated multiplication and solve.

45. $10^2 =$ _____ = _____

46. $10^5 =$ _____

         $=$ _____

47. $10^4 =$ _____

         $=$ _____

48. $10^1 =$ _____ = _____

Use an exponent to write each repeated multiplication.

49. $5 \times 10 \times 10 =$ _____

50. $3 \times 10 \times 10 \times 10 \times 10 =$ _____

51. $9 \times 10 \times 10 \times 10 =$ _____

52. $2 \times 10 =$ _____

53. $7 \times 10 \times 10 \times 10 \times 10 \times 10$

     $=$ _____

54. $1 \times 10 \times 10 =$ _____

► Multiply a Whole Number by a Power of Ten

Multiply 3 by powers of ten. Look for a pattern.

$3 \times 10^1 = 3 \times 10 = 30$

$3 \times 10^2 = 3 \times 10 \times 10 =$ _____

$3 \times 10^3 = 3 \times 10 \times 10 \times 10 =$ _____

$30 \times 10^3 = (3 \times 10) \times 10 \times 10 \times 10 =$ _____

55. What pattern do you see?

_____

_____

Find the value.

56. $1 \times 10^4 =$ _____   **57.** $2 \times 10^3 =$ _____   **58.** $62 \times 10^2 =$ _____

Complete the pattern.

59. $7 \times 10^1 = 7 \times 10 =$ _____

$7 \times 10^2 = 7 \times 100 =$ _____

$7 \times 10^3 = 7 \times 1,000 =$ _____

$7 \times 10^4 = 7 \times 10,000 =$ _____

60. $9 \times 10^1 =$ _____ $= 90$

$9 \times 10^2 =$ _____ $= 900$

$9 \times 10^3 =$ _____ $= 9,000$

$9 \times 10^4 =$ _____ $= 90,000$

61. $65 \times 10^1 = 65 \times 10 =$ _____

$65 \times 10^2 = 65 \times 100 =$ _____

$65 \times 10^3 = 65 \times 1,000 =$ _____

$65 \times 10^4 = 65 \times 10,000 =$ _____

62. $523 \times 10^1 =$ _____ $= 5,230$

$523 \times 10^2 = 523 \times 100 =$ _____

$523 \times 10^3 =$ _____ $= 523,000$

$523 \times 10^4 = 523 \times 10,000 =$ _____

63. $14 \times 10^1 = 14 \times 10 =$ _____

$14 \times 10^2 = 14 \times 100 =$ _____

$14 \times 10^3 = 14 \times 1,000 =$ _____

$14 \times 10^4 = 14 \times 10,000 =$ _____

64. $108 \times 10^1 =$ _____ $= 1,080$

$108 \times 10^2 = 108 \times 100 =$ _____

$108 \times 10^3 =$ _____ $= 108,000$

$108 \times 10^4 = 108 \times 10,000 =$ _____

► Patterns with Fives

Dear Math Students,

I know that when you multiply two numbers together, the product has the same number of zeros as the two factors. For example, 60 × 20 is 1,200. There are two zeros in the factors (60 and 20) and two zeros in the product (1,200).

I am confused about one thing. I know that 50 × 2 is 100, and I am quite sure that 50 × 4 is 200. In these two problems, there is only one zero in the factors, but there are **two** zeros in the product. The pattern I learned does not seem to be true in these cases.

Did I make a mistake somewhere?

Thank you.
Puzzled Penguin

1. Write an answer to Puzzled Penguin.

_____

_____

_____

2. Find each product to complete the chart below. One factor in each problem contains a 5. Discuss the patterns you see for the number of zeros in each product. How does the number of zeros in the product relate to the number of zeros in the factors?

_____

_____

5 × 20	=	5 × 2 × 10	=	10 × 10	=
50 × 40	=	5 × 10 × 4 × 10	=	20 × 100	=
50 × 600	=	5 × 10 × 6 × 100	=	30 × 1,000	=
500 × 800	=	5 × 100 × 8 × 100	=	40 × 10,000	=

3. Find each product to complete the chart below. Again, one factor in each problem contains a 5. How does the number of zeros in the product relate to the number of zeros in the factors?

_____

_____

5×30	=	$5 \times 3 \times 10$	=	15×10	=
50×50	=	$5 \times 10 \times 5 \times 10$	=	25×100	=
50×700	=	$5 \times 10 \times 7 \times 100$	=	$35 \times 1,000$	=
500×900	=	$5 \times 100 \times 9 \times 100$	=	$45 \times 10,000$	=

4. Explain why the product sometimes has an "extra" zero.

_____

_____

▶ Solve Fives-Pattern Problems

Decide how many zeros there will be. Then solve.

5. $\begin{array}{r} 80 \\ \times\ 5 \\ \hline \end{array}$
  6. $\begin{array}{r} 70 \\ \times\ 5 \\ \hline \end{array}$
  7. $\begin{array}{r} 90 \\ \times\ 50 \\ \hline \end{array}$
  8. $\begin{array}{r} 60 \\ \times\ 50 \\ \hline \end{array}$

Write an equation. Then solve.

9. Ernesto and his sister Dora are playing a computer game. Ernesto has earned 200 points so far. His sister has earned 50 times as many points. How many points has Dora earned?

_____

10. Mount Katahdin is the tallest mountain in Maine. It is about 5,000 feet tall. Mount McKinley is the tallest mountain in the United States. It is four times as tall as Mount Katahdin. About how tall is Mount McKinley?

_____

Name _____   **Date** _____

CA CC Content Standards 5.NBT.1, 5.NBT.5
Mathematical Practices MP.1, MP.2, MP.4, MP.6

▶ Solve with Place Value Sections

Think about finding the area of this rectangle
(*Area = length × width*). It would be difficult to find
43 × 67 in one step, but if you broke the rectangle
into smaller **Place Value Sections**, then you could do it.

When you multiply larger numbers, you often need to
break the problem into smaller parts. The products of
these smaller parts are called **partial products**. After you
find all the partial products, you can add them together.

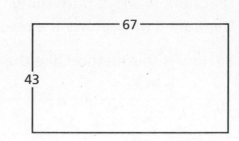

1. A flower garden is 67 inches long and 43 inches wide. What
   is the area of the garden? Explain how Place Value Sections
   are used to solve the problem below.

43 × 67	60	+ 7
40	40 × 60 = 2,400	40 × 7 = 280	40
+ 3	3 × 60 = 180	3 × 7 = 21	+ 3
	60	+ 7

_____

_____

2. A theater has 39 rows of seats. Each row has 54 seats.
   How many seats are in the theater? Use Place Value
   Sections to solve the multiplication problem below.

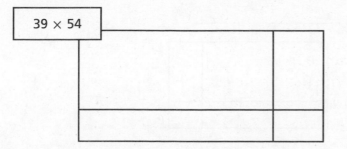

39 × 54

© Houghton Mifflin Harcourt Publishing Company

Name _____ **Date** _____

VOCABULARY
Expanded Notation

► Numerical Methods for Multiplication

Look at the **Expanded Notation** method of solving 43 × 67 below.
Diagrams A and B both show the Expanded Notation method.
Diagram B only shows the results of the steps.

3. How is this method like the Place Value Sections? How is it different?

_____

_____

_____

_____

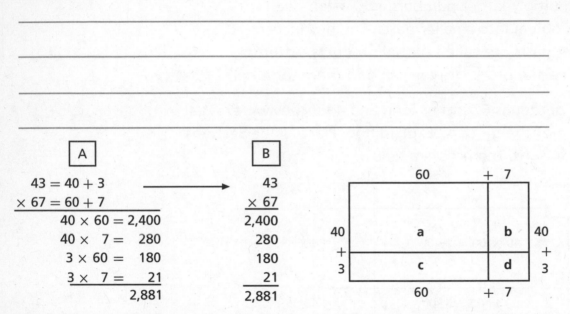

4. The rectangle above shows the same problem as Diagrams A and B. Match each
   section (a, b, c, d) to the 4 partial products shown in the Expanded
   Notation method above.

Solve. Use any method you like.

Show your work.

5. There are 32 cattle cars on today's
   train to Detroit. Each car holds
   28 cows. How many cows are on
   the train?

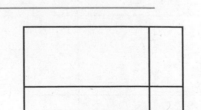

_____

6. Mr. Brooks is planning to carpet
   his office. The office is 21 feet long
   and 52 feet wide. How much carpet
   does he need if he carpets
   the entire room?

_____

The Area Model for Multiplication

Name _____

Date _____

CA CC Content Standards 5.NBT.5
Mathematical Practices MP.3, MP.6, MP.7

▶ Methods for Two-Digit Multiplication

Look at the multiplication problem shown here. It is solved with another place value method called **Place Value Rows**.

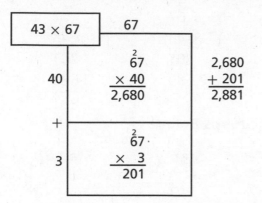

1. Explain the steps of the Place Value Rows method.

   _____

   _____

   _____

   _____

2. How is the Place Value Rows method alike and different from the Place Value Sections method?

   _____

   _____

   _____

Use the Place Value Rows method to solve each problem.

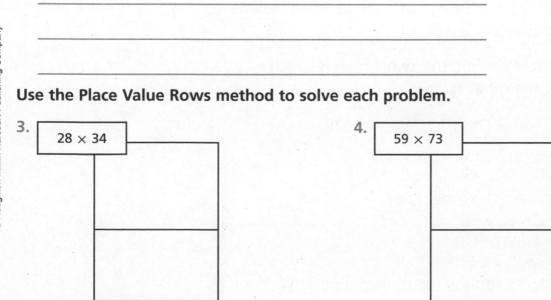

3. | 28 × 34 |

4. | 59 × 73 |

VOCABULARY
New Groups Below
Short Cut

Here, 43 × 67 is solved with a method we call
the **Short Cut**.

Step 1	**Step 2**	**Step 3**	**Step 4**	**Step 5**	**Step 6**
²67	²67	²67	²²67	²²67	²²67
× 43	× 43	× 43	× 43	× 43	× 43
1	201	201	201	201	201
		0	80	2,680	2,680
					2,881

Here, 43 × 67 is solved with a method we call **New Groups Below**.

Step 1	**Step 2**	**Step 3**	**Step 4**	**Step 5**	**Step 6**
67	67	67	67	67	67
× 43	× 43	× 43	× 43	× 43	× 43
²1	¹²81	¹²81	¹²81	¹²81	¹²81
		0	²80	²²480	²²480
					¹2,881

5. **Discuss** How is the Short Cut method different from
   the New Groups Below method?

6. **Discuss** How is the Short Cut method like the
   Place Value Rows method? How is it different?

The Place Value Rows and Short Cut methods both make
use of the Distributive Property.

In each, one factor is broken into two addends which
are multiplied by the other factor.

$$67 \times 43 = 67(40 + 3)$$

$$= (67 \times 40) + (67 \times 3)$$

$$= (2,680) + (201)$$

$$= 2,881$$

7. Use another 2-digit by 2-digit multiplication problem
   to illustrate how to use the Distributive Property.

-4
Class Activity

Name _____   Date _____

► Discuss Multiplication Methods

Below are the four multiplication methods your class has tried.
Discuss these questions about the methods.

7. How do the 4 partial products in the two top methods relate
   to the 2 partial products in the two bottom methods?

8. The Short Cut method starts with the ones. Could we do
   the other methods by starting with the ones? Explain
   why or why not.

Place Value Sections

Expanded Notation

$$67 = 60 + 7$$
$$43 = 40 + 3$$
$$40 \times 60 = 2,400$$
$$40 \times 7 = 280$$
$$3 \times 60 = 180$$
$$3 \times 7 = 21$$
$$2,881$$

Place Value Rows

Short Cut

New Groups Above   **New Groups Below**

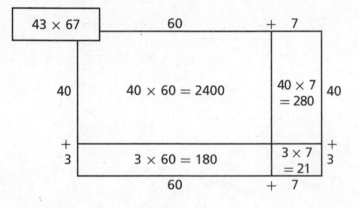

Solve.

9.   94
    × 36

10.   73
    × 45

11.   69
    × 82

© Houghton Mifflin Harcourt Publishing Company

PATH to FLUENCY Practice Multiplying Multidigit Numbers

Solve. Use any method.

12. 42
   × 5

13. 37
   × 9

14. 742
   × 4

15. 5,553
   × 2

16. 204
   × 6

17. 7,128
   × 7

18. 54
   × 3

19. 385
   × 8

20. 24
   × 15

21. 28
   × 92

22. 54
   × 47

23. 35
   × 29

24. 27
   × 29

25. 71
   × 43

26. 63
   × 85

27. 38
   × 50

28. 83
   × 83

29. 17
   × 71

30. 44
   × 55

31. 75
   × 16

▶ Solve Real World Problems

Show your work.

32. Max rode his bike 44 miles every week for 28 weeks.
    How many miles did he ride altogether?

_____

33. Monique wants to cover a watercolor painting with glass.
    The painting is 25 inches long and 35 inches wide.
    What is the area of the glass needed for the painting?

_____

Multiply Two-Digit Numbers

Name _____   **Date** _____

CA CC Content Standards 5.NBT.5
Mathematical Practices MP.6

PATH to FLUENCY Practice Multiplying

Multiply.

1. 54
   × 7

2. 508
   × 6

3. 945
   × 8

4. 2,786
   × 3

5. 643
   × 4

6. 5,433
   × 2

7. 1,079
   × 7

8. 400
   × 50

9. 49
   × 76

10. 65
    × 24

11. 40
    × 40

12. 53
    × 35

13. 27
    × 98

14. 33
    × 88

15. 71
    × 28

16. 92
    × 47

17. 21
    × 29

18. 47
    × 37

19. 44
    × 44

20. 54
    × 75

▶ Solve Real World Problems

Solve.

Show your work.

21. Pascal wants to read 99 pages every week for 35 weeks.
How many pages will he have read by the end of that time?
How could he use mental math to find the solution?

_____

_____

22. Jenny's garden is 28 feet by 50 feet. What is the area of her
garden? How could she use mental math to find the area?

_____

_____

23. Padma has a dining room table whose top is 42 inches wide
and 72 inches long. What is the area of the top of her table?

_____

24. The drama club is making punch to sell at the school play.
Each batch uses 64 fluid ounces of fruit juice. If they plan to
make 18 batches, how much fruit juice will they need?

_____

Write an equation and then solve.

25. Tigers living in Siberia can have home ranges from 190 to
1,500 square miles depending on how plentiful their prey is.
If a tiger's range is in the shape of a rectangle that is 47 miles
wide by 29 miles long, what is the area of its home range?

_____

26. Paul and John have a stamp collection. They keep their stamps
in an album that has 54 pages. There are 24 stamps on each
side of each page. How many stamps are in their collection?

_____

Practice Multiplication

▶ Decimals in Money Situations

The Ruiz children had a yard sale. They sold some old toys.
They made a table to show how many toys they sold and
how much money they earned.

Number of Items	Item Price	Total Earned in Cents	Total Earned in Dollars
3 jump ropes	9 cents	3 × 9 cents = 27 cents	3 × $0.09 = $0.27
4 marbles	2 cents	4 × 2 cents = 8 cents	4 × $0.02 = $0.08
6 toy cars	12 cents	6 × 12 cents = 72 cents	6 × $0.12 = $0.72
5 puzzles	30 cents	5 × 30 cents = 150 cents	5 × $0.30 = $1.50

1. How did they know the number of decimal places in each
   product in the last column?

   _____

2. How much money did they earn in dollars?

   _____

Mia saves the change from her lunch money each day.
She gets $0.34 in change, and she has been saving it for
26 days. Mia used the steps below to find how much
money she has saved so far.

$0.34 = $0.30 + $0.04
× 26 =   20 +   6

Step 1	Multiply by the number in the ones place (6).	6 × $0.04 = 6 × 4 cents = 24 cents = 6 × $0.30 = 6 × 30 cents = 180 cents =	$0.24 $1.80
Step 2	Multiply by the number in the tens place (2 tens = 20).	20 × $0.04 = 20 × 4 cents = 80 cents = 20 × $0.30 = 20 × 30 cents = 60 dimes =	_____ _____
Step 3	Add the partial products.		_____

3. How many decimal places are there in the decimal factor
   (0.34)? How many decimal places are there in the answer?

   _____

© Houghton Mifflin Harcourt Publishing Company

Name _____ Date _____

► Decimals in Money Situations (continued)

A bead factory spends $0.65 to make each crystal bead. The steps below show how Antonio finds the total amount the factory spends to make 222 crystal beads.

$0.65
× 222

Step 1	Multiply by the number in the ones place.	2 × $0.65 = _____
Step 2	Multiply by the number in the tens place. (2 tens = 20; 1.30 shifts 1 place left.)	20 × $0.65 = _____
Step 3	Multiply by the number in the hundreds place. (2 hundreds = 200; 1.30 shifts 2 places left.)	200 × $0.65 = _____
Step 4	Add the partial products.	_____

4. How many decimal places are there in the decimal factor (0.65)? How many decimal places are there in the answer?

_____

_____

5. Describe the relationship between the number of decimal places you have seen in a decimal product and the number of decimal places in its decimal factor.

_____

_____

6. The owners of the Seven Seas Spice Company want to sell twice as much spice in the future as they do now. The table shows how much spice they sell in a week now and how much they want to sell in the future. Show how to get the answers by adding.

Cloves	0.3 ton	2 × 0.3 ton = 0.6 ton	because 0.3 + 0.3 = 0.6
Cinnamon	0.04 ton	2 × 0.04 ton = 0.08 ton	because 0.04 + _____ = _____
Ginger	0.07 ton	2 × 0.07 ton = 0.14 ton	because _____ + _____ = _____
Pepper	0.6 ton	2 × 0.6 ton = 1.2 tons	because _____ + _____ = _____

7. Look at the number of decimal places in each decimal factor and the number of decimal places in each product. What pattern do you see?

_____

_____

8. Is this the same pattern you saw in Problems 1–4?

_____

_____

Multiply Decimals with Whole Numbers

▶ Practice Multiplying with Decimals

Find each product.

9. $\begin{array}{r} 0.8 \\ \times\ 6 \\ \hline \end{array}$

10. $\begin{array}{r} 0.3 \\ \times\ 40 \\ \hline \end{array}$

11. $\begin{array}{r} 0.05 \\ \times\ 9 \\ \hline \end{array}$

12. $\begin{array}{r} 0.14 \\ \times\ 32 \\ \hline \end{array}$

13. $\begin{array}{r} 0.43 \\ \times\ 64 \\ \hline \end{array}$

14. $\begin{array}{r} 0.27 \\ \times\ 31 \\ \hline \end{array}$

15. $\begin{array}{r} 0.7 \\ \times\ 333 \\ \hline \end{array}$

16. $\begin{array}{r} 0.2 \\ \times\ 421 \\ \hline \end{array}$

17. $\begin{array}{r} 0.11 \\ \times\ 219 \\ \hline \end{array}$

18. $\begin{array}{r} 0.67 \\ \times\ 102 \\ \hline \end{array}$

19. $\begin{array}{r} 1.03 \\ \times\ 15 \\ \hline \end{array}$

20. $\begin{array}{r} 2.15 \\ \times\ 35 \\ \hline \end{array}$

21. $\begin{array}{r} 3.25 \\ \times\ 25 \\ \hline \end{array}$

22. $\begin{array}{r} 6.01 \\ \times\ 19 \\ \hline \end{array}$

23. $\begin{array}{r} 2.03 \\ \times\ 111 \\ \hline \end{array}$

Solve.

Show your work.

24. Jesse bought 3 aquariums. Each holds 8.75 gallons of water. How many gallons of water will they hold altogether?

_____

25. Jesse wants to buy 24 angelfish. Each angelfish costs $2.35. What will be the total cost of the angelfish?

_____

26. There are three goldfish in one of Jesse's aquariums. Gus is the smallest. He weighs only 0.98 ounce. Ella weighs 3 times as much as Gus. What is Ella's weight?

_____

© Houghton Mifflin Harcourt Publishing Company

► Zero Patterns in Decimal Places

You have seen patterns in multiplying by multiples of 10.
You have seen patterns in multiplying by decimals. You can use
these two patterns together. The table below shows how you
can multiply decimals by whole numbers, using:

- ones, tens, and hundreds
- tenths, hundredths, and thousandths

x	0.3	0.03	0.003
2	2×0.3 $= 2 \times 3 \times 0.1$ $= 6 \times 0.1$ $= 0.6$	2×0.03 $= 2 \times 3 \times 0.01$ $= 6 \times 0.01$ $= 0.06$	2×0.003 $= 2 \times 3 \times 0.001$ $= 6 \times 0.001$ $= 0.006$
20	20×0.3 $= 2 \times 10 \times 3 \times 0.1$ $= 60 \times 0.1$ $= 6.0$	20×0.03 $= 2 \times 10 \times 3 \times 0.01$ $= 60 \times 0.01$ $= 0.60$	20×0.003 $= 2 \times 10 \times 3 \times 0.001$ $= 60 \times 0.001$ $= 0.060$
200	200×0.3 $= 2 \times 100 \times 3 \times 0.1$ $= 600 \times 0.1$ $= 60.0$	200×0.03 $= 2 \times 100 \times 3 \times 0.01$ $= 600 \times 0.01$ $= 6.00$	200×0.003 $= 2 \times 100 \times 3 \times 0.001$ $= 600 \times 0.001$ $= 0.600$

Find each product using the method shown in the table above.

27. $4 \times 0.2 =$ _____

28. $5 \times 0.6 =$ _____

39. $40 \times 0.07 =$ _____

30. $300 \times 0.3 =$ _____

31. $200 \times 0.08 =$ _____

Name _____ **Date** _____

CA CC Content Standards 5.NBT.1, 5.NBT.2, 5.NBT.7
Mathematical Practices MP.1, MP.2, MP.3, MP.6, MP.7, MP.8

▶ **Shifts with Decimals**

Leon earns $213 a month. The money is shown
here. He will save some of it every month.

Leon's Earnings

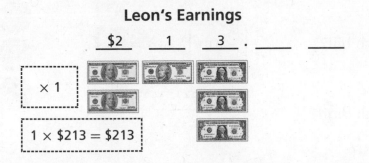

$$1 \times \$213 = \$213$$

Answer the questions about the different savings plans.

1. If he saves 0.1 of his earnings, how much
   will he save each month?

   _____

2. What happens to the value of each bill?

   _____

3. What happens to the value of each digit?

   _____

4. When you multiply by 0.1, does each digit
   shift to the right or left?

   _____

5. How many places does each digit shift?

   _____

Save 0.1 Each Month

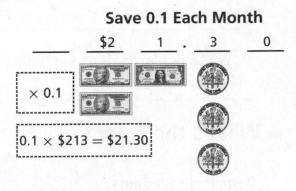

$$0.1 \times \$213 = \$21.30$$

▶ Shifts with Decimals (continued)

6. If he saves 0.01 of his earnings, how much will he save each month?

_____

7. What happens to the value of each bill?

_____

8. What happens to the value of each digit?

_____

9. When you multiply by 0.01, does each digit shift to the right or left?

_____

10. How many places does each digit shift?

_____

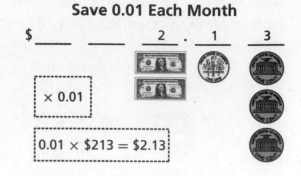

Save 0.01 Each Month

$ ____ ____ 2 . 1 3

× 0.01

0.01 × $213 = $2.13

▶ What's the Error?

Dear Math Students,

Today I went to the bank to deposit $345.00. When I told the banker this was 0.1 of $34.50, he told me that I'd made a mistake.

Can you tell me what I did wrong?

Your friend,
Puzzled Penguin

11. Write a response to Puzzled Penguin.

_____

_____

_____

Multiply by Decimals

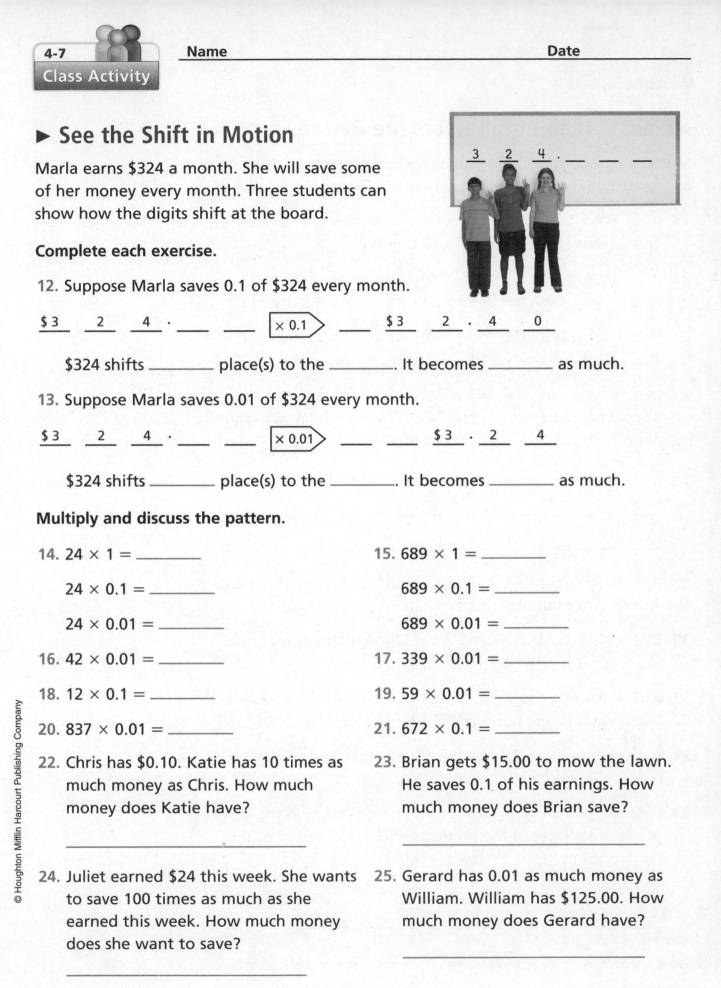

▶ See the Shift in Motion

Marla earns $324 a month. She will save some of her money every month. Three students can show how the digits shift at the board.

$\underline{3} \quad \underline{2} \quad \underline{4} \cdot \underline{\quad} \underline{\quad} \underline{\quad} \underline{\quad}$

Complete each exercise.

12. Suppose Marla saves 0.1 of $324 every month.

$\$3 \underline{\quad} 2 \underline{\quad} 4 \cdot \underline{\quad} \underline{\quad}$ [$\times 0.1$⟩ $\underline{\quad} \$3 \underline{\quad} 2 \cdot 4 \cdot 0$

$324 shifts _____ place(s) to the _____. It becomes _____ as much.

13. Suppose Marla saves 0.01 of $324 every month.

$\$3 \underline{\quad} 2 \underline{\quad} 4 \cdot \underline{\quad} \underline{\quad}$ [$\times 0.01$⟩ $\underline{\quad} \underline{\quad} \$3 \cdot 2 \underline{\quad} 4$

$324 shifts _____ place(s) to the _____. It becomes _____ as much.

Multiply and discuss the pattern.

14. $24 \times 1 =$ _____

$24 \times 0.1 =$ _____

$24 \times 0.01 =$ _____

15. $689 \times 1 =$ _____

$689 \times 0.1 =$ _____

$689 \times 0.01 =$ _____

16. $42 \times 0.01 =$ _____

17. $339 \times 0.01 =$ _____

18. $12 \times 0.1 =$ _____

19. $59 \times 0.01 =$ _____

20. $837 \times 0.01 =$ _____

21. $672 \times 0.1 =$ _____

22. Chris has $0.10. Katie has 10 times as much money as Chris. How much money does Katie have?

_____

23. Brian gets $15.00 to mow the lawn. He saves 0.1 of his earnings. How much money does Brian save?

_____

24. Juliet earned $24 this week. She wants to save 100 times as much as she earned this week. How much money does she want to save?

_____

25. Gerard has 0.01 as much money as William. William has $125.00. How much money does Gerard have?

_____

▶ Shifts When Both Factors Are Decimals

Multiply by one tenth. Think about what it means to take one tenth of another part. You can think about money.

26. 0.1 × 0.4 = _____ Think: What is one tenth of one tenth? Then, what is one tenth of four tenths?

27. 0.1 × 0.04 = _____ Think: What is one tenth of one hundredth? Then, what is one tenth of four hundredths?

28. How many places did the 4 shift each time you multiplied? _____ In which direction? _____

29. Look at your answers. What pattern do you see in the number of decimal places in the products? How is it related to the number of places in the two factors?

_____

_____

_____

Multiply by one hundredth. Think about what it means to take one hundredth of another part.

30. 0.01 × 4 = _____ Think: What is one hundredth of one? Then, what is one hundredth of four?

31. 0.01 × 0.4 = _____ Think: What is one hundredth of one tenth? Then, what is one hundredth of four tenths?

32. How many places did the 4 shift each time you multiplied? _____ In which direction? _____

33. Look at your answers. What pattern do you see in the number of decimal places in the products? How is it related to the number of places in the two factors?

_____

_____

_____

▶ Shifts When Both Factors Are Decimals (continued)

34. How could you express the generalization about the number of decimal places in the product when you multiply a decimal number by another decimal number? Is it the same as the generalization for multiplying a decimal number by a whole number?

_____

_____

_____

_____

35. To multiply by 2 tenths or 2 hundredths, you could think of 2 tenths as 2 × 0.1 and 2 hundredths as 2 × 0.01.

0.2 × 0.4 = (2 × _____) × 0.4 = 2 × (0.1 × 0.4) = 2 × 0.04 = _____

0.02 × 0.4 = (2 × _____) × 0.4 = 2 × (0.01 × 0.4) = 2 × 0.004 = _____

Is your generalization about the number of decimal places in the product still true? _____

Use the shift pattern to solve each multiplication. Check to see if the generalization works.

36. 0.2 × 0.4 = _____   **37.** 0.2 × 0.04 = _____

38. 2 × 0.4 = _____   **39.** 0.02 × 0.4 = _____

40. 0.4
      × 6

41. 0.04
      × 6

42. 0.4
      × 0.6

43. 0.4
      × 0.06

44. 0.05
      × 3

45. 0.13
      × 2

46. 1.2
      × 3

47. 0.2
      × 0.6

▶ Shifts When Both Factors Are Decimals (continued)

Using the generalization you just discovered, solve each multiplication.

48. $0.3 \times 0.4 =$ _____

49. $0.3 \times 0.04 =$ _____

50. $0.03 \times 0.4 =$ _____

51. $3 \times 0.4 =$ _____

52. $\begin{array}{r} 0.05 \\ \times\ 5 \\ \hline \end{array}$

53. $\begin{array}{r} 0.9 \\ \times\ 0.3 \\ \hline \end{array}$

54. $\begin{array}{r} 0.07 \\ \times\ 0.3 \\ \hline \end{array}$

55. $\begin{array}{r} 0.4 \\ \times\ 0.08 \\ \hline \end{array}$

56. $\begin{array}{r} 0.4 \\ \times\ 5 \\ \hline \end{array}$

57. $\begin{array}{r} 0.3 \\ \times\ 1.3 \\ \hline \end{array}$

58. $\begin{array}{r} 0.2 \\ \times\ 0.26 \\ \hline \end{array}$

59. $\begin{array}{r} 0.7 \\ \times\ 4.2 \\ \hline \end{array}$

Solve.

Show your work.

60. Benjamin bought 6.2 pounds of rice. Each pound cost $0.90. How much did he spend on rice?

_____

61. Sabrina walks 0.85 mile to school. Kirk walks only 0.3 as far as Sabrina. How far does Kirk walk to school?

_____

62. Isabel wrote 4 letters to her pen pals. For each letter she bought a stamp. Each stamp cost $0.60. How much did she spend on stamps?

_____

63. Maura rode her bike 5 laps around the block. Each lap is 0.45 mile. How many miles did she ride?

_____

64. Kim bought 2 pounds of baked turkey that cost $5.98 per pound. What was the total cost?

_____

▶ Practice Multiplying Decimal Numbers Greater Than 1

Multiply.

1. 2.6 × 0.7	3. 8.23 × 0.6	3. 7.21 × 0.3	4. 8.7 × 0.53
5. 4.7 × 6.3	6. 5.4 × 5.2	7. 0.43 × 1.8	8. 7.01 × 0.2
9. 1.04 × 0.4	10. 8.6 × 3.9	11. 5.7 × 1.7	12. 8.2 × 7.4
13. 4.6 × 0.12	14. 8.5 × 8.5	15. 246.1 × .09	16. 7.7 × 3.2
17. 1.1 × 0.11	18. 4.3 × 2.4	19. 7.8 × 0.15	20. 3.8 × 4.5

▶ **Solve Real World Problems**

Solve.   *Show your work.*

21. Maggie is training to run in a 6-mile race. Her training
    program has her increase her weekly long run each week.
    This week she ran 4.5 miles. Next week she will run 1.3 times
    as far as she did this week. How far will she run next week?

    _____

22. Hank earned $140.95. Pellam earned 0.8 times as much as
    Hank did. How much did Pellam earn?

    _____

23. Tariq is building his dog a bed. He wants the width of his
    dog's bed to be .75 times as long as the length. If the length
    is 1.5 meters, how wide will the bed be?

    _____

24. The door to Sophia's room is 0.9 m wide and 2.06 m tall.
    In order to buy paint to paint it, she needs to know the area of
    one side of the door. What is the area of one side of her door?

    _____

Write an equation and then solve.

25. Adrienne and Evelyn have a pet cat. When they got it as a kitten,
    it weighed 0.6 kilograms. Now it weighs 7.3 times as much as it
    did when it was a kitten. How much does their cat weigh now?

    _____

26. The official weight of a U.S. penny is 2.5 grams. A quarter
    weighs a little more than 2.2 times as much as a penny.
    About how much does a quarter weigh?

    _____

    _____

► Multiplication Properties

The **Commutative Property of Multiplication**, **Associative Property of Multiplication**, and **Distributive Property** can help you multiply.

Properties	
Commutative Property of Multiplication	$a \times b = b \times a$
Associative Property of Multiplication	$(a \times b) \times c = a \times (b \times c)$
Distributive Property	$a \times b + a \times c = a \times (b + c)$

Complete the equation and name the property used.

27. $4.5 \times 3.2 =$ _____ $\times\ 4.5$

_____

28. $80 \times (72 \times 38) = ($_____ $\times\ 72) \times 38$

_____

29. $7 \times (3.8 + 4.2) = (7 \times$ _____ $) + (7 \times 4.2)$

_____

30. $40 \times (50 \times 1.13) = (40 \times 50) \times$ _____

_____

31. $(3.2 \times 8.1) + (3.2 \times 1.9) =$ _____ $\times (8.1 + 1.9)$

_____

32. $0.98 \times 2.6 = 2.6 \times$ _____

_____

33. Explain how you might use the properties to
solve $25 \times (5.7 \times 4)$ mentally.

_____

_____

_____

▶ Multiplication Properties (continued)

34. Explain how you might use the properties to solve
$(3.7 \times 8.2) + (1.8 \times 3.7)$ mentally.

_____

_____

35. Your calculator's battery is dead and you have to solve
this problem; $4 \times (7.3 \times 0.25)$. How can you make this
multiplication problem easier to solve?

_____

_____

_____

▶ What's the Error?

Dear Math Students,

I need to solve this problem; $4 \times (2.5 \times 9.3)$.

I rewrote the problem using the Associative
Property of Multiplication to make it easier to
multiply;

$(4 \times 2.5) \times 9.3 = 10 \times 9.3 = 0.93$.
That answer doesn't seem right. Can you help
me find my error

Your friend,
Puzzled Penguin

36. Write a response to Puzzled Penguin.

_____

_____

_____

► Compare Whole Number and Decimal Multipliers

Complete each sentence.

Whole Number Multipliers	Decimal Number Multipliers

1. When you multiply by 10, the number gets _____ times as great. The digits shift _____ place(s) to the _____.

2. When you multiply by 0.1, the number gets _____ as great. The digits shift _____ place(s) to the _____.

3. When you multiply by 100, the number gets _____ times as great. The digits shift _____ place(s) to the _____.

4. When you multiply by 0.01, the number gets _____ as great. The digits shift _____ place(s) to the _____.

5. How is multiplying by 10 or 100 like multiplying by 0.1 or 0.01? How is it different?

_____

_____

_____

For each exercise, discuss the shift. Then find each product.

6. 3.6 × 10	7. 3.6 × 0.1	8. 3.6 × 100	9. 3.6 × 0.01
10. 0.48 × 10	11. 5.6 × 0.01	12. 2.49 × 0.1	13. 1.7 × 100
14. 0.6 × 0.2	15. 0.9 × 300	16. 0.9 × 0.04	17. 0.6 × 60

Name _____ Date _____

▶ Patterns in Multiplication by Powers of 10 Using Exponents

Recall that powers of 10, such as 10^1, 10^2, and 10^3 represent repeated multiplication with 10. The exponent tells you how many times to use 10 as a factor. The number of times 10 is used as a factor tells you how many places to shift the digits.

$10^1 = 10 \qquad 10^2 = 10 \times 10 = 100 \qquad 10^3 = 10 \times 10 \times 10 = 1,000$

$0.4 \times 10 = 0.4 \times 10^1 = \underline{\quad 4 \quad}$

$0.4 \times 100 = 0.4 \times 10 \times 10 = 0.4 \times 10^2 = \underline{\quad 40 \quad}$

$0.4 \times 1,000 = 0.4 \times 10 \times 10 \times 10 = 0.4 \times 10^3 = \underline{\quad 400 \quad}$

Study the pattern above. Then complete Exercises 18–25.

18. $0.8 \times 10 = 0.8 \times 10^1 = \underline{\qquad}$ **19.** $0.27 \times 10 = 0.27 \times 10^1 = \underline{\qquad}$

$0.8 \times 100 = 0.8 \times 10^2 = \underline{\qquad}$ $0.27 \times 100 = 0.27 \times 10^2 = \underline{\qquad}$

$0.8 \times 1,000 = 0.8 \times 10^3 = \underline{\qquad}$ $0.27 \times 1,000 = 0.27 \times 10^3 = \underline{\qquad}$

20. $4.8 \times 10^1 = \underline{\qquad}$ **21.** $6.23 \times 10^1 = \underline{\qquad}$ **22.** $0.49 \times 10^1 = \underline{\qquad}$

$4.8 \times 10^2 = \underline{\qquad}$ $6.23 \times 10^2 = \underline{\qquad}$ $0.49 \times 10^2 = \underline{\qquad}$

$4.8 \times 10^3 = \underline{\qquad}$ $6.23 \times 10^3 = \underline{\qquad}$ $0.49 \times 10^3 = \underline{\qquad}$

23. $1.3 \times 10^1 = \underline{\qquad}$ **24.** $0.84 \times 10^1 = \underline{\qquad}$ **25.** $0.51 \times \underline{\qquad} = 5.1$

$1.3 \times 10^2 = \underline{\qquad}$ $0.84 \times \underline{\qquad} = 84$ $0.51 \times 10^2 = \underline{\qquad}$

$1.3 \times \underline{\qquad} = 1,300$ $0.84 \times 10^3 = \underline{\qquad}$ $0.51 \times 10^3 = \underline{\qquad}$

26. How is multiplying 0.07 by 10^2 like multiplying 7 by 10^2? How is it different?

_____

_____

_____

Compare Shift Patterns

► What's the Error?

Dear Math Students,

My friend said that I didn't correctly complete the three equations shown below.

$6.08 \times 10^1 = 6.8$ $6.08 \times 10^2 = 68$ $6.08 \times 10^3 = 680$

What error did I make? Please help me find the correct products.

Your friend,
Puzzled Penguin

27. Write an answer to Puzzled Penguin.

_____

_____

_____

Dear Math Students,

My teacher said that $0.8 \text{ kg} = 0.8 \times 10^3 \text{ g}$. When I calculated how many grams that is, she said I had done it incorrectly. My answer was $0.8 \text{ kg} = 824 \text{ g}$.

If I estimate the product, 0.8 times 100 is 80 so my answer seems reasonable. What error did I make? Please help me find the correct product.

Your friend,
Puzzled Penguin

28. Write an answer to Puzzled Penguin.

_____

_____

_____

▶ Extend and Apply the Generalization

Zeros at the end of a decimal number do not change the value of the number. Remember this as you explore the generalization about the number of decimal places in a product.

These exercises all have an "extra" zero in the product because of the 5-pattern. **Complete each multiplication.**

29. $0.5 \times 2 =$ _____   30. $0.08 \times 0.5 =$ _____   31. $0.4 \times 0.5 =$ _____

32. Does the generalization about the product having the same number of decimal places as the two factors still work? _____

These problems are all the same, but are expressed in different ways. **Multiply.**

33. $3 \times 3 =$ _____   34. $3.0 \times 3 =$ _____   35. $3.0 \times 3.0 =$ _____

36. Does the generalization about the product having the same number of decimal places as the two factors still work? Do your answers all represent the same amount? _____

37.   40
    × 0.23

38.   0.02
    × 0.3

39.   400
    × 0.6

40.   60
    × 1.7

41. Ada and her family are canoeing in the wilderness. They carry the canoe along trails between lakes. Their map gives each trail distance in rods. They know that a rod is equal to 5.5 yards. Find each trail distance in yards.

    Show your work.

    Black Bear Trail; 8 rods _____

    Dark Cloud Trail; 24.1 rods _____

42. One of the world's largest diamonds is the Star of Africa, which is 530.2 carats. A carat is about 0.2 gram. What is the mass of the Star of Africa in grams?

▶ Review of Rounding

Round each number.

1. Round 42 to the nearest ten. Which ten is closer to 42?

_____

50 ⌐
42
40 ⌐

2. Round 762 to the nearest hundred. Which hundred is closer to 762?

_____

800 ⌐
762
700 ⌐

3. Round 0.86 to the nearest tenth. Which tenth is closer to 0.86?

_____

0.9 ⌐
0.86
0.8 ⌐

4. Round 0.263 to the nearest hundredth. Which hundredth is closer to 0.263?

_____

0.27 ⌐
0.263
0.26 ⌐

Round to the nearest ten.

5. 46 _____ **6.** 71 _____ **7.** 85 _____ **8.** 928 _____

Round to the nearest hundred.

9. 231 _____ **10.** 459 _____ **11.** 893 _____ **12.** 350 _____

Round to the nearest tenth.

13. 0.73 _____ **14.** 0.91 _____ **15.** 0.15 _____ **16.** 0.483 _____

Round to the nearest hundredth.

17. 0.532 _____ **18.** 0.609 _____ **19.** 0.789 _____ **20.** 0.165 _____

21. What is the greatest whole number that can be rounded to 30? What is the least?

_____

22. What is the greatest decimal in hundredths that can be rounded to 14.5? What is the least?

_____

▶ Explore Estimation in Multiplication

For each exercise, round the factors and multiply mentally to find the estimated answer. After finding all the estimated answers, go back and find each exact answer.

Estimated Answer   **Exact Answer**

23. $24 \times 39 \approx$ _____ $\times$ _____ $\approx$ _____ $24 \times 39 =$ _____

24. $151 \times 32 \approx$ _____ $\times$ _____ $\approx$ _____ $151 \times 32 =$ _____

25. $0.74 \times 0.2 \approx$ _____ $\times$ _____ $\approx$ _____ $0.74 \times 0.2 =$ _____

26. $12.3 \times 3.7 \approx$ _____ $\times$ _____ $\approx$ _____ $12.3 \times 3.7 =$ _____

27. Is there more than one way to round these numbers? Why are some exact answers closer to the estimated answer than others?

_____

_____

_____

▶ Use Estimation to Check Answers

28. Tanya did these multiplications on her calculator.

$24.5 \times 4 = 98$ $0.56 \times 30 = 1.68$ $15.2 \times 2.03 = 30.856$

$0.09 \times 143 = 12.87$ $0.74 \times 12.2 = 90.28$ $9.03 \times 6.9 = 623.07$

How can she use estimation to see if each answer makes sense? Which answers are clearly wrong?

_____

_____

_____

_____

_____

▶ Practice with Decimals

Suppose you know that 23 × 48 = 1,104. Use this to find each product.

1. 23 × 4.8 = _____

2. 0.23 × 4.8 = _____

3. 2.3 × 4.8 = _____

4. 0.48 × 2.3 = _____

5. 48 × 2.3 = _____

6. 4.8 × 2.3 = _____

7. 23 × 0.48 = _____

8. 48 × 0.23 = _____

Find each product.

9.   46
   × 0.9

10.   75
   × 0.8

11.   97
   × 0.04

12.   64
   × 0.05

13. 0.34
   × 12

14.   59
   × 0.28

15.   4.5
   × 7.3

16. 0.92
   × 0.8

17. 0.08
   × 0.6

18. 0.53
   × 0.4

19.   7.6
   × 0.3

20.   0.2
   × 0.04

► Solve Word Problems

Write an equation. Then solve. Check that your answers are reasonable.

Show your work.

21. Marcus sails his boat 4.5 miles every day. If he sails for 25 days, how far will he travel in all?

_____

22. The distance around a circle (the circumference) is about 3.14 times the diameter. If a circular table has a diameter of 3 feet, what is the circumference?

_____

23. Nina is reading about red kangaroos. She found out that a male red kangaroo usually weighs about 66 kilograms, and a female red kangaroo usually weighs about 26.5 kilograms. One kilogram is about 2.2 pounds. What is the weight of a male red kangaroo in pounds?

_____

24. The 5th grade is getting a special lunch to celebrate the end of the first grading period. The cafeteria manager is planning to buy 0.3 pound of turkey for each student. If turkey is on sale for $0.79 per pound, what will it cost to give turkey to 100 students?

_____

25. One U.S. gallon of water weighs 8.3 pounds. How much would 4.8 gallons weigh?

_____

26. Guadalupe read an article that said the cost of driving a car 1 mile was about 57.5¢. She lives 0.6 mile from school. If the article is correct, what does it cost to drive Guadalupe to and from school every school day for a week?

_____

▶ Math and Insects

Insects are sometimes called bugs, and are the most numerous living things on Earth.

There are nearly one million different kinds of known insects, and most scientists believe more than that number of insects have never been discovered and given names.

The table below shows typical lengths, in centimeters and inches, of interesting insects.

Emperor Dragonfly

Insect	Length	
	cm	in.
crazy ant	0.25	0.1
green stinkbug	1.5	0.6
walkingstick	25	10
megachile pluto bee	3.8	1.5
spotless ladybug	0.5	0.2
emperor dragonfly	7.8	3.1
praying mantis	10	4
giant water bug	11.6	4.6
firefly	1.9	0.75

Walkingstick Insect
Show your work.

Solve. Use the table above.

1. Eight green stinkbugs, marching one behind the other, are about the same length in inches as which insect?

   _____

2. In centimeters, which insect is about forty times as long as a crazy ant?

   _____

3. The total length in inches of fifty spotless ladybugs is about the same length as which insect?

   _____

The table below shows typical
wingspans, in centimeters and inches,
of interesting flying insects.

Buckeye Butterfly

Insect	wingspan	
	cm	in.
confused cloudywing butterfly	3.2	1.26
Atlas moth	28	11.0
monarch butterfly	9	3.5
sleepy orange butterfly	4.5	1.8
damselfly	19.1	7.5
parasitic wasp	0.15	0.06
chickweed geometer moth	2.25	0.9
buckeye butterfly	5.7	2.24

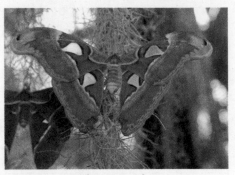

Atlas Moth

Solve. Use the table above.

Show your work.

4. In centimeters, which wingspan is twice as long as the
   wingspan of a chickweed geometer moth?

   _____

5. In inches, the total wingspan of six confused cloudywing
   butterflies is about the same as the wingspan of which insect?

   _____

6. How does the total wingspan in centimeters of 60 parasitic
   wasps compare to the wingspan of 2 sleepy orange butterflies?

   _____

7. An Atlas moth has a wingspan of 11 inches. Suppose the
   moth was placed on the cover of your math book. What is
   the difference between the length of the wingspan and your book?

   _____

8. Write and solve a problem of your own using data from the table.

   _____

   _____

Focus on Mathematical Practices

1. Classify each product as being equal to 43, equal to 430, or equal to 4,300. Write the letter of the product in the correct box.

A 43×10^2	B 43×10^1	C 4.3×10^2
D 0.43×10^2	E 4.3×10^1	F 4.3×10^3

43	430	4,300

2. Hakeem puts $59 from each paycheck into his savings account. He gets paid every two weeks or 26 times per year. His goal is to save $1,500 this year. Will Hakeem reach his goal? Explain your answer using words, a model, and an equation.

3. Choose one factor from each column that will result in a product with three zeros.

○ 2		○ 0.4
○ 20	×	○ 4
○ 200		○ 40
○ 2,000		○ 400

4. Select each product that is correct. Mark all that apply.

   (A) $300 \times 60 = 18,000$

   (B) $30 \times 800 = 240$

   (C) $27 \times 100 = 2,700$

   (D) $60 \times 10 = 6,000$

Name _____   Date _____

5. Select each item with a product equal to 260. Mark all that apply.

   (A) 2.6×10^2

   (B) 26×10^3

   (C) 0.26×10^3

   (D) 2.6×10^1

   (E) 26×10^2

6. Write a decimal to complete the equation.

   $$7 \times 0.04 = 7 \times 4 \times \underline{\hspace{1cm}}$$

7. Ben says that the product 50×60 should have two zeros. Sharlene says the product should have three zeros.

   Part A

   Which student is correct? What is the product of 50×60?

   Part B

   How do you know?

8. Order the products from least to greatest by writing each expression in a box.

| 500 × 30 | 3 × 50 | 5 × 0.03 | 50 × 0.3 | 300 × 5 |

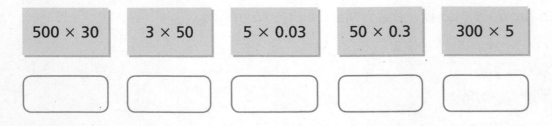

9. Select the expression that is equivalent to
   8 × 10 × 10 × 10. Mark all that apply.

   (A) 8 × 10²

   (B) 80 × 10²

   (C) 8 × 10³

   (D) 8 × (3 × 10)

   (E) 800 × 10¹

   (F) 8 × 100

10. An Atlas moth has a wingspan of 11 inches. What is the
    wingspan of 26 Atlas moths?

    _____ inches

11. Jodi's best score on a video game is 50 points. Mark's best
    score on the game is 1.5 times as much as Jodi's best score.

    Part A

    How many points did Mark score on the video game?

    _____ points

    Part B

    Virginia's best score is only 0.6 times Jodi's best score.
    How many points did Virginia score on the game?

    _____ points

12. Myra is painting a 76 inch by 22 inch mural along the gym
    wall. How many square inches will she paint? Write the
    numbers in the boxes that will complete the model and
    then solve.

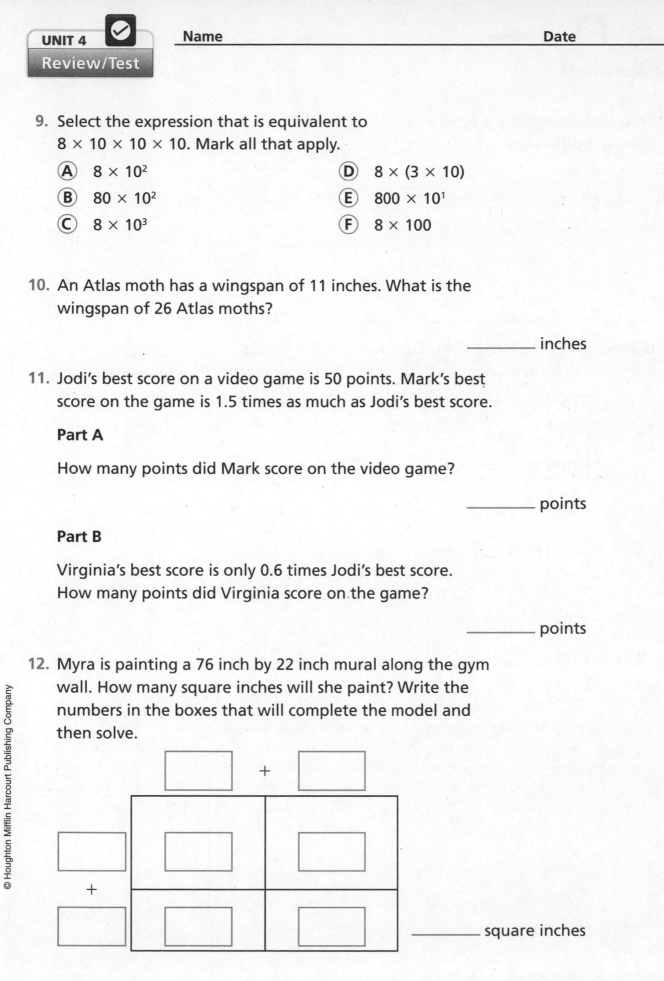

    _____ square inches

Name _____ Date _____

13. How is multiplying 0.3 by 10 like multiplying 0.3 by 0.1?
How is it different?

For numbers 14a–14c, circle the correct value in the box to
make the equation true.

14a. $0.76 \times$ $\begin{array}{c} 10^1 \\ 10^2 \\ 10^3 \end{array}$ $= 760$

14b. $0.76 \times$ $\begin{array}{c} 10^1 \\ 10^2 \\ 10^3 \end{array}$ $= 76$

14c. $0.76 \times$ $\begin{array}{c} 10^1 \\ 10^2 \\ 10^3 \end{array}$ $= 7.6$

15. Describe how the digits shift when you multiply a number
by 0.1.

Name _____   Date _____

16. Write the numbers that complete the word problem. Some numbers are not used.

$202.50	3	1.5	$16.75	$20.25
2.5	4	$4.50	$3.20	$2.025

Tamira buys _____ pounds of mixed nuts each day for _____ days.

The nuts cost _____ per pound. She pays _____ for all the mixed nuts.

17. Write the letter of the expression next to the number that shows its product.

A 82 × 0.7   ☐ 0.592

B 0.6 × 92   ☐ 59.2

C 8.2 × 0.7   ☐ 5.74

D 0.8 × 74   ☐ 55.2

E 9.2 × 0.06   ☐ 57.4

F 7.4 × 0.08   ☐ 0.552

18. A walkingstick is 2.5 times as long as a praying mantis. If a praying mantis is 10 centimeters long, how long is a walkingstick?

_____ centimeters

19. Choose the word or phrase that makes the sentence true.

When you multiply by 100, each digit shifts

to the | right | by | one place |
       | left | | two places |
       | | | three places |

© Houghton Mifflin Harcourt Publishing Company

20. Multiply 7,952 × 8. Explain how you know your answer is reasonable.

21. Select the products that are correct. Mark all that apply.

   (A) 0.01 × 600 = 60,000

   (B) 300 × 0.1 = 30

   (C) 0.01 × 20 = 0.2

   (D) 90 × 0.1 = 0.9

22. Eve worked during the summer as a lifeguard. She earns $16 per hour. How much does Eve earn if she works 28 hours? Show your work.

Show your work.

23. Mr. Clemente measured 29.7 grams of potassium chloride for each of 7 lab groups in his chemistry class. How much potassium chloride did Mr. Clemente measure?

   _____ grams

24. When you multiply 24.7 by 0.1, is the answer greater than or less than 24.7? Explain.

Reference Tables

Table of Measures	
Metric	**Customary**
Length/Area/Volume	

Length/Area/Volume

Metric

1 millimeter (mm) = 0.001 meter (m)

1 centimeter (cm) = 0.01 meter

1 decimeter (dm) = 0.1 meter

1 dekameter (dam) = 10 meters

1 hectometer (hm) = 100 meters

1 kilometer (km) = 1,000 meters

1 hectare (ha) = 1,000 square meters (m²)

1 square centimeter = 1 sq cm
A metric unit for measuring area. It is the area of a square that is 1 centimeter on each side.

1 cubic centimeter = 1 cu cm
A unit for measuring volume. It is the volume of a cube with each edge 1 centimeter long.

Customary

1 foot (ft) = 12 inches (in.)

1 yard (yd) = 36 inches

1 yard = 3 feet

1 mile (mi) = 5,280 feet

1 mile = 1,760 yards

1 acre = 4,840 square yards

1 acre = 43,560 square feet

1 acre = $\frac{1}{640}$ square mile

1 square inch = 1 sq in.
A customary unit for measuring area. It is the area of a square that is 1 inch on each side.

1 cubic inch = 1 cu in.
A unit for measuring volume. It is the volume of a cube with each edge 1 inch long.

Capacity

Metric

1 milliliter (mL) = 0.001 liter (L)

1 centiliter (cL) = 0.01 liter

1 deciliter (dL) = 0.1 liter

1 dekaliter (daL) = 10 liters

1 hectoliter (hL) = 100 liters

1 kiloliter (kL) = 1,000 liters

Customary

1 teaspoon (tsp) = $\frac{1}{6}$ fluid ounce (fl oz)

1 tablespoon (tbsp) = $\frac{1}{2}$ fluid ounce

1 cup (c) = 8 fluid ounces

1 pint (pt) = 2 cups

1 quart (qt) = 2 pints

1 gallon (gal) = 4 quarts

Mass / Weight

Mass

1 milligram (mg) = 0.001 gram (g)

1 centigram (cg) = 0.01 gram

1 decigram (dg) = 0.1 gram

1 dekagram (dag) = 10 grams

1 hectogram (hg) = 100 grams

1 kilogram (kg) = 1,000 grams

1 metric ton = 1,000 kilograms

Weight

1 pound (lb) = 16 ounces

1 ton (T) = 2,000 pounds

Volume/Capacity/Mass for Water

1 cubic centimeter = 1 milliliter = 1 gram

1,000 cubic centimeters = 1 liter = 1 kilogram

Reference Tables (continued)

Table of Units of Time

Time

1 minute (min) = 60 seconds (sec)

1 hour (hr) = 60 minutes

1 day = 24 hours

1 week (wk) = 7 days

1 month is about 30 days

1 year (yr) = 12 months (mo)
or about 52 weeks

1 year = 365 days

1 leap year = 366 days

1 decade = 10 years

1 century = 100 years

1 millennium = 1,000 years

Table of Formulas

Perimeter

Polygon P = sum of the lengths of the sides

Rectangle $P = 2(l + w)$ or $P = 2l + 2w$

Square $P = 4s$

Area

Rectangle $A = l \cdot w$

Square $A = s \cdot s$ or $A = s^2$

Volume of a Rectangular Prism

$V = lwh$ or $V = Bh$

(where B is the area of the base of the prism)

Properties of Operations

Associative Property of Addition

$(a + b) + c = a + (b + c)$ $(2 + 5) + 3 = 2 + (5 + 3)$

Commutative Property of Addition

$a + b = b + a$ $4 + 6 = 6 + 4$

Additive Identity Property of 0

$a + 0 = 0 + a = a$ $3 + 0 = 0 + 3 = 3$

Associative Property of Multiplication

$(a \cdot b) \cdot c = a \cdot (b \cdot c)$ $(3 \cdot 5) \cdot 7 = 3 \cdot (5 \cdot 7)$

Commutative Property of Multiplication

$a \cdot b = b \cdot a$ $6 \cdot 3 = 3 \cdot 6$

Multiplicative Identity Property of 1

$a \cdot 1 = 1 \cdot a = a$ $8 \cdot 1 = 1 \cdot 8 = 8$

Multiplicative Inverse

For every $a \neq 0$ there exists $\frac{1}{a}$ so that $a \cdot \frac{1}{a} = \frac{1}{a} \cdot a = 1$.

For $a = 5$, $5 \cdot \frac{1}{5} = \frac{1}{5} \cdot 5 = 1$.

Distributive Property of Multiplication over Addition

$a \cdot (b + c) = (a \cdot b) + (a \cdot c)$ $2 \cdot (4 + 3) = (2 \cdot 4) + (2 \cdot 3)$

Order of Operations

Step 1 Perform operations inside parentheses.

Step 2 Simplify powers.*

Step 3 Multiply and divide from left to right.

Step 4 Add and subtract from left to right.

*Grade 5 does not include simplifying expressions with exponents.

Problem Types

Addition and Subtraction Problem Types

	Result Unknown	Change Unknown	Start Unknown
Add to	A glass contained $\frac{2}{3}$ cup of orange juice. Then $\frac{1}{4}$ cup of pineapple juice was added. How much juice is in the glass now? *Situation and solution equation:*[1] $\frac{2}{3} + \frac{1}{4} = c$	A glass contained $\frac{2}{3}$ cup of orange juice. Then some pineapple juice was added. Now the glass contains $\frac{11}{12}$ cup of juice. How much pineapple juice was added? *Situation equation:* $\frac{2}{3} + c = \frac{11}{12}$ *Solution equation:* $c = \frac{11}{12} - \frac{2}{3}$	A glass contained some orange juice. Then $\frac{1}{4}$ cup of pineapple juice was added. Now the glass contains $\frac{11}{12}$ cup of juice. How much orange juice was in the glass to start? *Situation equation* $c + \frac{1}{4} = \frac{11}{12}$ *Solution equation:* $c = \frac{11}{12} - \frac{1}{4}$
Take from	Micah had a ribbon $\frac{5}{6}$ yard long. He cut off a piece $\frac{1}{3}$ yard long. What is the length of the ribbon that is left? *Situation and solution equation:* $\frac{5}{6} - \frac{1}{3} = r$	Micah had a ribbon $\frac{5}{6}$ yard long. He cut off a piece. Now the ribbon is $\frac{1}{2}$ yard long. What is the length of the ribbon he cut off? *Situation equation:* $\frac{5}{6} - r = \frac{1}{2}$ *Solution equation:* $r = \frac{5}{6} - \frac{1}{2}$	Micah had a ribbon. He cut off a piece $\frac{1}{3}$ yard long. Now the ribbon is $\frac{1}{2}$ yard long. What was the length of the ribbon he started with? *Situation equation:* $r - \frac{1}{3} = \frac{1}{2}$ *Solution equation:* $r = \frac{1}{2} + \frac{1}{3}$

[1]A situation equation represents the structure (action) in the problem situation. A solution equation shows the operation used to find the answer.

	Total Unknown	Addend Unknown	Both Addends Unknown
Put Together/ Take Apart	A baker combines $\frac{3}{4}$ cup of white flour and $\frac{1}{2}$ cup of wheat flour. How much flour is this altogether? *Math drawing:*[2] 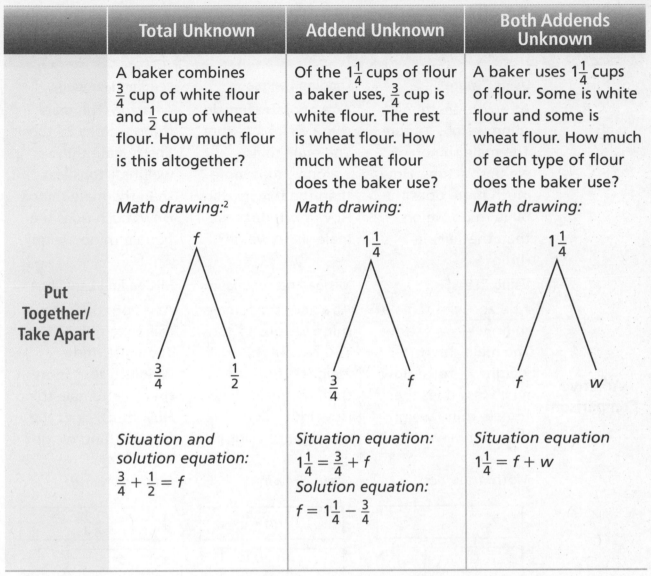 *Situation and solution equation:* $\frac{3}{4} + \frac{1}{2} = f$	Of the $1\frac{1}{4}$ cups of flour a baker uses, $\frac{3}{4}$ cup is white flour. The rest is wheat flour. How much wheat flour does the baker use? *Math drawing:* *Situation equation:* $1\frac{1}{4} = \frac{3}{4} + f$ *Solution equation:* $f = 1\frac{1}{4} - \frac{3}{4}$	A baker uses $1\frac{1}{4}$ cups of flour. Some is white flour and some is wheat flour. How much of each type of flour does the baker use? *Math drawing:* *Situation equation* $1\frac{1}{4} = f + w$

[2]These math drawings are called math mountains in Grades 1–3 and break-apart drawings in Grades 4 and 5.

Problem Types continued

Problem Types (continued)

Addition and Subtraction Problem Types

	Difference Unknown	Greater Unknown	Smaller Unknown
Additive Comparison[1]	**Using "More"** At a zoo, the female rhino weighs $1\frac{3}{4}$ tons. The male rhino weighs $2\frac{1}{2}$ tons. How much more does the male rhino weigh than the female rhino? **Using "Less"** At a zoo, the female rhino weighs $1\frac{3}{4}$ tons. The male rhino weighs $2\frac{1}{2}$ tons. How much less does the female rhino weigh than the male rhino?	**Leading Language** At a zoo, the female rhino weighs $1\frac{3}{4}$ tons. The male rhino weighs $\frac{3}{4}$ tons more than the female rhino. How much does the male rhino weigh? **Misleading Language** At a zoo, the female rhino weighs $1\frac{3}{4}$ tons. The female rhino weighs $\frac{3}{4}$ tons less than the male rhino. How much does the male rhino weigh?	**Leading Language** At a zoo, the male rhino weighs $2\frac{1}{2}$ tons. The female rhino weighs $\frac{3}{4}$ tons less than the male rhino. How much does the female rhino weigh? **Misleading Language** At a zoo, the male rhino weighs $2\frac{1}{2}$ tons. The male rhino weighs $\frac{3}{4}$ tons more than the female rhino. How much does the female rhino weigh?
	Math drawing: 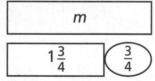 Situation equation: $1\frac{3}{4} + d = 2\frac{1}{2}$ or $d = 2\frac{1}{2} - 1\frac{3}{4}$ Solution equation: $d = 2\frac{1}{2} - 1\frac{3}{4}$	*Math drawing:* (drawing: m over $1\frac{3}{4}$ and $\frac{3}{4}$) Situation and solution equation: $1\frac{3}{4} + \frac{3}{4} = m$	*Math drawing:* 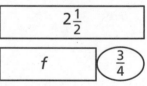 Situation equation $f + \frac{3}{4} = 2\frac{1}{2}$ or $f = 2\frac{1}{2} - \frac{3}{4}$ Solution equation: $f = 2\frac{1}{2} - \frac{3}{4}$

[1]A comparison sentence can always be said in two ways. One way uses *more*, and the other uses *fewer* or *less*. Misleading language suggests the wrong operation. For example, it says the *female rhino weighs $\frac{3}{4}$ tons less than the male*, but you have to add $\frac{3}{4}$ tons to the female's weight to get the male's weight

© Houghton Mifflin Harcourt Publishing Company

Multiplication and Division Problem Types[1]

	Unknown Product	Group Size Unknown	Number of Groups Unknown
Equal Groups	Maddie ran around a $\frac{1}{4}$-mile track 16 times. How far did she run? *Situation and solution equation:* $n = 16 \cdot \frac{1}{4}$	Maddie ran around a track 16 times. She ran 4 miles in all. What is the distance around the track? *Situation equation:* $16 \cdot n = 4$ *Solution equation:* $n = 4 \div 16$	Maddie ran around a $\frac{1}{4}$-mile track. She ran a total distance of 4 miles. How many times did she run around the track? *Situation equation* $n \cdot \frac{1}{4} = 4$ *Solution equation:* $n = 4 \div \frac{1}{4}$

	Unknown Product	Unknown Factor	Unknown Factor
Arrays[2]	An auditorium has 58 rows with 32 seats in each row. How many seats are in the auditorium? *Math drawing:* 32 58 | s *Situation and solution equation:* $s = 58 \cdot 32$	An auditorium has 58 rows with the same number of seats in each row. There are 1,856 seats in all. How many seats are in each row? *Math drawing:* s 58 | 1,856 *Situation equation:* $58 \cdot s = 1,856$ *Solution equation:* $s = 1,856 \div 58$	The 1,856 seats in an auditorium are arranged in rows of 32. How many rows of seats are there? *Math drawing:* 32 s | 1,856 *Situation equation* $s \cdot 32 = 1,856$ *Solution equation:* $s = 1,856 \div 32$

[1]In Grade 5, students solve three types of fraction division problems: 1) They divide two whole numbers in cases where the quotient is a fraction; 2) They divide a whole number by a unit fraction; 3) They divide a unit fraction by a whole number. Fraction division with non-unit fractions is introduced in Grade 6.

[2]We use rectangle models for both array and area problems in Grades 5 and 6 because the numbers in the problems are too large to represent with arrays.

Problem Types (continued)

Multiplication and Division Problem Types

	Unknown Product	Unknown Factor	Unknown Factor
Area	A poster has a length of 1.2 meters and a width of 0.7 meter. What is the area of the poster? *Math drawing:* 1.2 0.7 | A | *Situation and solution equation:* $A = 1.2 \cdot 0.7$	A poster has an area of 0.84 square meters. The length of the poster is 1.2 meters. What is the width of the poster? *Math drawing:* 1.2 w | 0.84 | *Situation equation:* $1.2 \cdot w = 0.84$ *Solution equation:* $w = 0.84 \div 1.2$	A poster has an area of 0.84 square meters. The width of the poster is 0.7 meter. What is the length of the poster? *Math drawing:* l 0.7 | 0.84 | *Situation equation* $l \cdot 0.7 = 0.84$ *Solution equation:* $l = 0.84 \div 0.7$

	Unknown Product	Unknown Factor	Unknown Factor
Multiplicative Comparison	**Whole Number Multiplier** Sam has 5 times as many goldfish as Brady has. Brady has 3 goldfish. How many goldfish does Sam have? *Math drawing:* s: 3 3 3 3 3 b: 3 *Situation and solution equation:* $s = 5 \cdot 3$	**Whole Number Multiplier** Sam has 5 times as many goldfish as Brady has. Sam has 15 goldfish. How many goldfish does Brady have? *Math drawing:* 15 s b *Situation equation:* $5 \cdot b = 15$ *Solution equation:* $b = 15 \div 5$	**Whole Number Multiplier** Sam has 15 goldfish. Brady has 3 goldfish. The number of goldfish Sam has is how many times the number Brady has? *Math drawing:* 15 s: 3 3 3 3 3 b: 3 *Situation equation* $n \cdot 3 = 15$ *Solution equation:* $n = 15 \div 3$
	Fractional Multiplier Brady has $\frac{1}{5}$ times as many goldfish as Sam has. Sam has 15 goldfish. How many goldfish does Brady have? *Math drawing:* 15 s b $\frac{1}{5}$ of 15 *Situation and solution equation:* $b = \frac{1}{5} \cdot 15$	**Fractional Multiplier** Brady has $\frac{1}{5}$ times as many goldfish as Sam has. Brady has 3 goldfish. How many goldfish does Sam have? *Math drawing:* s b: 3 $\frac{1}{5}$ of s *Situation equation:* $\frac{1}{5} \cdot s = 3$ *Solution equation:* $s = 3 \div \frac{1}{5}$	**Fractional Multiplier** Sam has 15 goldfish. Brady has 3 goldfish. The number of goldfish Brady has is how many times the number Sam has? *Math drawing:* 15 s: 3 3 3 3 3 b: 3 *Situation equation:* $n \cdot 15 = 3$ *Solution equation:* $n = 3 \div 15$

Vocabulary Activities

MathWord Power

▶ Word Review `PAIRS`

Work with a partner. Choose a word from a current unit or a review word from a previous unit. Use the word to complete one of the activities listed on the right. Then ask your partner if they have any edits to your work or questions about what you described. Repeat, having your partner choose a word.

Activities

▶ Give the meaning in words or gestures.

▶ Use the word in the sentence.

▶ Give another word that is related to the word in some way and explain the relationship.

▶ Crossword Puzzle `PAIRS` OR `INDIVIDUALS`

Create a crossword puzzle similar to the example below. Use vocabulary words from the unit. You can add other related words, too. Challenge your partner to solve the puzzle.

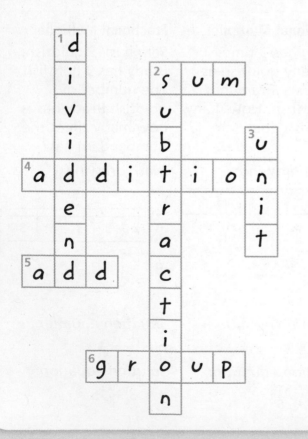

Across

2. The answer to an addition problem

4. _____ and subtraction are inverse operations.

5. To put amounts together

6. When you trade 10 ones for 1 ten, you _____.

Down

1. The number to be divided in a division problem

2. The operation that you can use to find out how much more one number is than another.

3. A fraction with a numerator of 1 is a _____ fraction.

▶ Word Wall   PAIRS OR SMALL GROUPS

With your teacher's permission, start a word wall in your classroom. As you work through each lesson, put the math vocabulary words on index cards and place them on the word wall. You can work with a partner or a small group to choose a word and give the definition.

▶ Word Web   INDIVIDUALS

Make a word web for a word or words you do not understand in a unit. Fill in the web with words or phrases that are related to the vocabulary word.

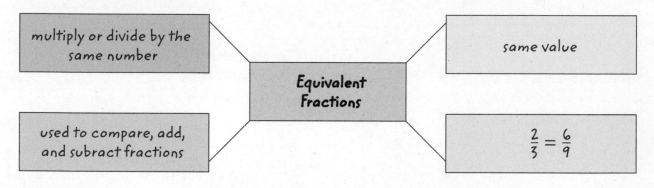

▶ Alphabet Challenge   PAIRS OR INDIVIDUALS

Take an alphabet challenge. Choose three letters from the alphabet. Think of three vocabulary words for each letter. Then write the definition or draw an example for each word.

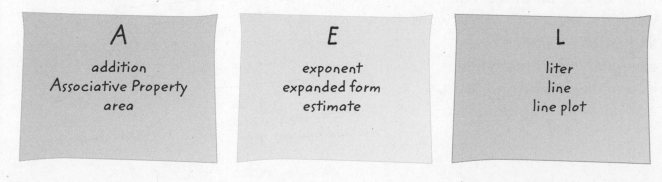

Vocabulary Activities (continued)

► Concentration PAIRS

Write the vocabulary words and related words from a unit on index cards. Write the definitions on a different set of index cards. Mix up both sets of cards. Then place the cards facedown on a table in an array, for example, 3 by 3 or 3 by 4. Take turns turning over two cards. If one card is a word and one card is a definition that matches the word, take the pair. Continue until each word has been matched with its definition.

area

The number of square units that cover a figure.

► Math Journal INDIVIDUALS

As you learn new words, write them in your Math Journal. Write the definition of the word and include a sketch or an example. As you learn new information about the word, add notes to your definition.

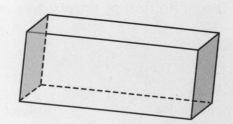

rectangular prism: a solid figure with two rectangular bases that are congruent and parallel

volume: a measure of the amount of space occupied by a solid figure

▶ What's the Word? PAIRS

Work together to make a poster or bulletin board display of
the words in a unit. Write definitions on a set of index cards.
Mix up the cards. Work with a partner, choosing a definition
from the index cards. Have your partner point to the word
on the poster and name the matching math vocabulary word.
Switch roles and try the activity again.

estimate

round

mixed number

equivalent fraction

common denominator

benchmark

simplify a fraction

unsimplify a fraction

unit fraction

a point of reference used for
comparing and estimating

Glossary

acute triangle A triangle with three acute angles.

Examples:

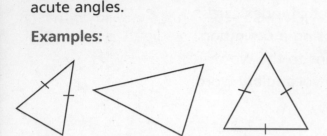

additive comparison A comparison in which one quantity is an amount greater or less than another. An additive comparison can be represented by an addition equation.

Example: Josh has 5 more goldfish than Tia.

$$j = t + 5$$

area The number of square units that cover a two-dimensional figure without gaps or overlap.

Example:

Area = 3 cm × 5 cm = 15 sq. cm

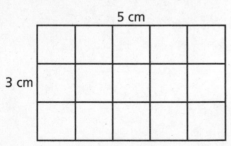

Associative Property of Addition Changing the grouping of addends does not change the sum. In symbols, $(a + b) + c = a + (b + c)$ for any numbers a, b, and c.

Example:

$(4.7 + 2.6) + 1.4 = 4.7 + (2.6 + 1.4)$

Associative Property of Multiplication Changing the grouping of factors does not change the product. In symbols, $(a \cdot b) \cdot c = a \cdot (b \cdot c)$ for any numbers a, b, and c.

Example:

$(0.73 \cdot 0.2) \cdot 5 = 0.73 \cdot (0.2 \cdot 5)$

base In a power, the number that is used as a repeated factor.

Example: In the power 10^3, the base is 10.

benchmark A point of reference used for comparing and estimating. The numbers 0, $\frac{1}{2}$, and 1 are common fraction benchmarks.

centimeter (cm) A unit of length in the metric system that equals one hundredth of a meter. 1 cm = 0.01 m.

closed shape A shape that starts and ends at the same point.

Examples:

common denominator A common multiple of two or more denominators.

Example: 18 is a common denominator of $\frac{2}{3}$ and $\frac{5}{6}$.

$$\frac{2}{3} = \frac{12}{18} \text{ and } \frac{5}{6} = \frac{15}{18}$$

Commutative Property of Addition
Changing the order of addends does not change the sum. In symbols, $a + b = b + a$ for any numbers a and b.

Example: $\frac{3}{5} + \frac{4}{9} = \frac{4}{9} + \frac{3}{5}$

Commutative Property of Multiplication Changing the order of factors does not change the product. In symbols, $a \cdot b = b \cdot a$ for any numbers a and b.

Example: $\frac{3}{7} \cdot \frac{4}{5} = \frac{4}{5} \cdot \frac{3}{7}$

comparison A statement, model, or drawing that shows the relationship between two quantities.

comparison bars Bars that represent the greater amount and the lesser amount in a comparison situation.

Example: Sarah made 2 quarts of soup. Ryan made 6 quarts. These comparison bars show that Ryan made 3 times as many quarts as Sarah.

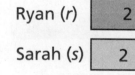

composite number A whole number that has more than two factors.

Example: The whole number 12 is a composite number because 1, 2, 3, 4, 6, and 12 are factors of 12.

composite solid A solid figure made by combining two or more basic solid figures.

Example: The composite solid on the left below is composed of two rectangular prisms, as shown on the right.

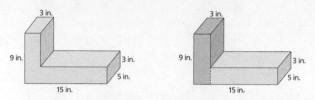

concave polygon A polygon for which you can connect two points inside the polygon with a segment that passes outside the polygon. A concave polygon has a "dent."

Examples:

convex polygon A polygon that is not concave. All the inside angles of a convex polygon have a measure less than 180°.

Examples:

Glossary (continued)

coordinate plane A system of coordinates formed by the perpendicular intersection of horizontal and vertical number lines.

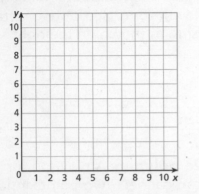

cubic unit The volume of a unit cube. A cubic unit is a unit for measuring volume.

D

decimal A number that includes a decimal point separating the whole number part of the number from the fraction part of the number.

Examples:

7.3	seven and three tenths
42.081	forty-two and eighty-one thousandths

decimeter (dm) A unit of length in the metric system that equals one tenth of a meter. 1 dm = 0.1 m.

Digit-by-Digit Method A method for solving division problems.

Example:

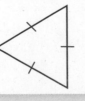

Distributive Property of Multiplication Over Addition

Multiplying a number by a sum gives the same result as multiplying the number by each addend and then adding the products. In symbols, for all numbers a, b, and c:

$$a \times (b + c) = a \times b + a \times c$$

Example:

$$4 \times (2 + 0.75) = 4 \times 2 + 4 \times 0.75$$

dividend The number that is divided in a division problem.

Example:

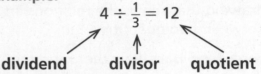

divisor The number you divide by in a division problem.

Example:

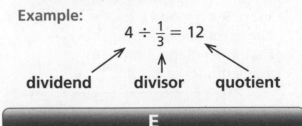

E

edge A line segment where two faces of a three-dimensional figure meet.

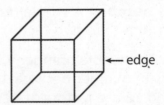

equilateral triangle A triangle with three sides of the same length.

Example:

equivalent decimals Decimals that represent the same value.

Example: 0.07 and 0.070 are equivalent decimals.

equivalent fractions Fractions that represent the same value.

Example: $\frac{1}{2}$ and $\frac{3}{6}$ are equivalent fractions.

estimate Find *about* how many or *about* how much, often by using rounding or benchmarks.

evaluate To substitute values for the variables in an expression and then simplify the resulting expression.

Example:

Evaluate $7 + 5 \cdot n$ for $n = 2$.

$7 + 5 \cdot n = 7 + 5 \cdot 2$ Substitute 2 for *n*.

$\qquad\qquad = 7 + 10$ Multiply.

$\qquad\qquad = 17$ Add

expanded form A way of writing a number that shows the value of each of its digits.

Example: The expanded form of 35.026 is $30 + 5 + 0.02 + 0.006$.

expanded form (powers of 10) A way of writing a number that shows the value of each of its digits using powers of 10.

Example: The expanded form of 35.026 using powers of 10 is

$(3 \times 10) + (5 \times 1) + (2 \times 0.01) + (6 + 0.001)$

Expanded Notation Method A method for solving multidigit multiplication and division problems.

Examples:

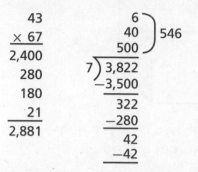

exponent In a power, the number that tells how many times the base is used as a factor.

Example: In the power 10^3, the exponent is 3.
$$10^3 = 10 \times 10 \times 10$$

exponential form The representation of a number that uses a base and an exponent.

Example: The exponential form of 100 is 10^2.

expression A combination of one or more numbers, variables, or numbers and variables, with one or more operations.

Examples: 4

$\qquad$ *t*

$\qquad$ $6 \cdot n$

$\qquad$ $4 \div p + 5$

$\qquad$ $5 \times 4 + 3 \times 7$

$\qquad$ $6 \cdot (x + 2)$

Glossary (continued)

F

face A flat surface of a three-dimensional figure.

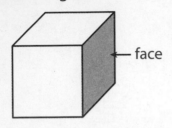

← face

factor One of two or more numbers multiplied to get a product.

Example:

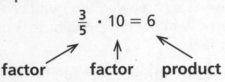

$$\frac{3}{5} \cdot 10 = 6$$

factor   factor   product

frequency table A table that shows how many times each outcome, item, or category occurs.

Example:

Outcome	Number of Students
1	6
2	3
3	5
4	4
5	2
6	5

G

greater than (>) A symbol used to show how two numbers compare. The greater number goes before the > symbol and the lesser number goes after.

Example: $\frac{2}{3} > \frac{1}{2}$ Two thirds is greater than one half.

H

hundredth A unit fraction representing one of one hundred equal parts of a whole, written as 0.01 or $\frac{1}{100}$.

I

isosceles triangle A triangle with at least two sides of the same length.

Examples:

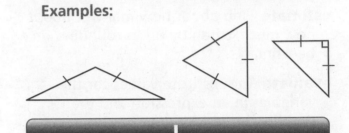

L

less than (<) A symbol used to show how two numbers compare. The lesser number goes before the < symbol and the greater number goes after.

Example: $\frac{1}{4} < \frac{1}{3}$ One fourth is less than one third.

line plot A diagram that uses a number line to show the frequency of data.

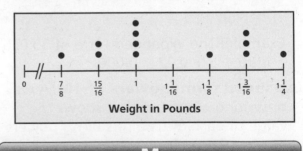

Weight in Pounds

M

meter The basic unit of length in the metric system.

mile (mi) A customary unit of length equal to 5,280 feet or 1,760 yards.

millimeter (mm) A unit of length in the metric system that equals one thousandth of a meter.
1 mm = 0.001 m.

mixed number A number with a whole number part and a fraction part.

Example: The mixed number $3\frac{2}{5}$ means $3 + \frac{2}{5}$.

multiplier The number the numerator and denominator of a fraction are multiplied by to get an equivalent fraction.

Example: A multiplier of 5 changes $\frac{2}{3}$ to $\frac{10}{15}$.

multiplicative comparison A comparison in which one quantity is a number of times the size of another. A multiplicative comparison can be represented by a multiplication equation or a division equation.

Example: Tomás picked 3 times as many apples as Catie.

$$t = 3 \cdot c$$

$$t \div 3 = c \text{ or } \frac{1}{3} \cdot t = c$$

N

New Groups Below Method A method used to solve multidigit multiplication problems.

Example:

```
        67
    ×   43
      1 2
        81
    2 2
      480
      1
    2,881
```

numerical pattern A sequence of numbers that share a relationship.

Example: In this numerical pattern, each term is 3 more than the term before.

2, 5, 8, 11, 14, . . .

O

obtuse triangle A triangle with an obtuse angle.

Examples:

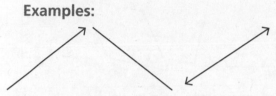

one-dimensional figure A figure with only one dimension, usually length.

Examples:

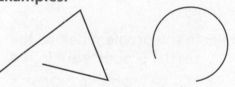

open shape A shape that does not start and end at the same point.

Examples:

Order of Operations A rule that states the order in which the operations in an expression should be done:

Step 1 Perform operations inside parentheses.

Step 2 Multiply and divide from left to right.

Step 3 Add and subtract from left to right.

ordered pair A pair of numbers that shows the position of a point on a coordinate plane.

Example: The ordered pair (3, 4) represents a point 3 units to the right of the y-axis and 4 units above the x-axis.

Glossary (continued)

origin The point (0, 0) on the coordinate plane.

overestimate An estimate that is too big.

P

parallelogram A quadrilateral with two pairs of parallel sides.

Examples:

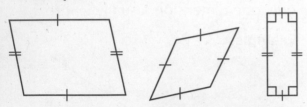

partial products In a multidigit multiplication problem, the products obtained by multiplying each place value of one factor by each place value of the other.

Example: In the problem below, the partial products are in red.

$$25 \cdot 53 = 20 \cdot 50 + 20 \cdot 3 + 5 \cdot 50 + 5 \cdot 3$$

perimeter The distance around a figure.

Example:

Perimeter = 2 · 3 cm + 2 · 5 cm = 16 cm

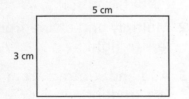

Place Value Rows Method A method used to solve multidigit multiplication problems.

Example:

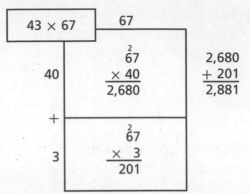

Place Value Sections Method A method used to solve multidigit multiplication and division problems.

Examples:

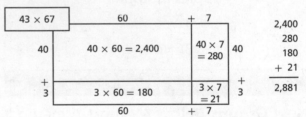

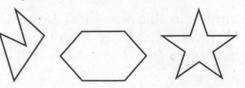

polygon A closed two-dimensional shape made from line segments that do not cross each other.

Examples:

power of 10 A power with a base of 10. A number in the form 10^n.

Examples: 10^1, 10^2, 10^3

prime number A whole number that has exactly two factors—the number itself and 1.

Examples: The whole number 13 is a prime number because the only factors of 13 are 1 and 13. The whole number 1 is neither prime nor composite.

product The result of a multiplication.

Example:

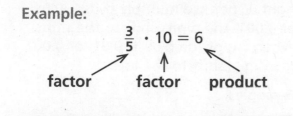

$$\frac{3}{5} \cdot 10 = 6$$

factor   factor   product

Q

quadrilateral A closed two-dimensional shape with four straight sides.

Examples:

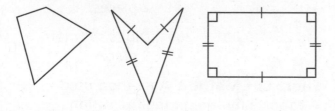

quotient The answer to a division problem.

Example:

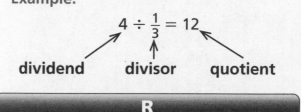

$$4 \div \frac{1}{3} = 12$$

dividend   divisor   quotient

R

rectangle A parallelogram with four right angles.

Examples:

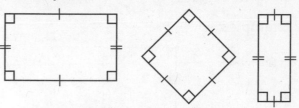

rectangular prism A solid figure with two rectangular bases that are congruent and parallel.

Example:

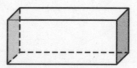

regular polygon A polygon in which all sides and all angles are congruent.

Examples:

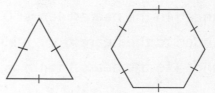

Glossary (continued)

remainder The number left over when a divisor does not divide evenly into a dividend.

Example:

$$
\begin{array}{r}
13 \\
7\overline{)94} \\
-7 \\
\hline
24 \\
21 \\
\hline
3 \leftarrow \text{remainder}
\end{array}
$$

rhombus A parallelogram with four congruent sides.

Examples:

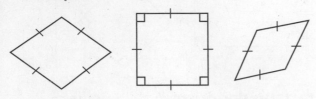

right triangle A triangle with a right angle.

Examples:

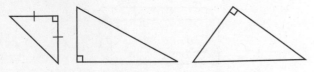

round To change a number to a nearby number.

Examples:

54.72 rounded to the nearest ten is 50.

54.72 rounded to the nearest one is 55.

54.72 rounded to the nearest tenth is 54.7.

$3\frac{7}{9}$ rounded to the nearest whole number is 4.

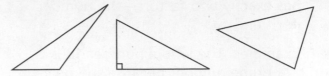

scalene triangle A triangle with no sides of the same length.

Examples:

shift To change position. When we multiply a decimal or whole number by 10, 100, or 1,000, the digits shift to the left. When we divide by 10, 100, or 1,000, the digits shift to the right. When we multiply by 0.1, 0.01, or 0.001, the digits shift to the right. When we divide by 0.1, 0.01, or 0.001, the digits shift to the left.

Examples:

$72.4 \times 100 = 7,240$ Digits shift left 2 places.

$5.04 \div 10 = 0.504$ Digits shift right 1 place.

$729 \times 0.01 = 7.29$ Digits shift right 2 places.

$0.26 \div 0.001 = 260$ Digits shift left 3 places.

Short Cut Method A method used to solve multidigit multiplication problems.

Example:

$$
\begin{array}{r}
\overset{1}{}\overset{2}{} \\
43 \\
\times 67 \\
\hline
301 \\
2,580 \\
\hline
2,881
\end{array}
$$

simplify a fraction Make an equivalent fraction by dividing the numerator and denominator of a fraction by the same number. Simplifying makes fewer but larger parts.

Example: Simplify $\frac{12}{16}$ by dividing the numerator and denominator by 4.

$$\frac{12 \div 4}{16 \div 4} = \frac{3}{4}$$

simplify an expression Use the Order of Operations to find the value of the expression.

Example: Simplify $6 \cdot (2 + 5) \div 3$.

$$6 \cdot (2 + 5) \div 3 \;\; = 6 \cdot 7 \div 3$$
$$= 42 \div 3$$
$$= 14$$

situation equation An equation that shows the action or the relationship in a word problem.

Example:

Liam has some change in his pocket. He spends 25¢. Now he has 36¢ in his pocket. How much change did he have to start?

situation equation: $x - 25 = 36$

solution equation An equation that shows the operation to perform in order to solve a word problem.

Example:

Liam has some change in his pocket. He spends 25¢. Now he has 36¢ in his pocket. How much change did he have to start?

solution equation: $x = 36 + 25$

square A rectangle with four congruent sides. (Or, a rhombus with four right angles.)

Examples:

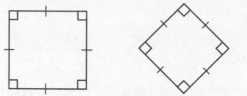

standard form The form of a number using digits, in which the place of each digit indicates its value.

Example: 407.65

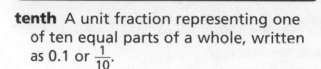

T

tenth A unit fraction representing one of ten equal parts of a whole, written as 0.1 or $\frac{1}{10}$.

term Each number in a numerical pattern.

Example: In the pattern below, 3 is the first term, and 9 is the fourth term.

3, 5, 7, 9, 11, . . .

thousandth A unit fraction representing one of one thousand equal parts of a whole, written as 0.001 or $\frac{1}{1,000}$.

three-dimensional figure A figure with three dimensions, usually length, width, and height.

Examples:

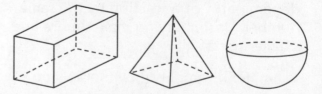

Glossary (continued)

ton (T) A customary unit of weight that equals 2,000 pounds.

trapezoid A quadrilateral with exactly one pair of parallel sides.

Examples:

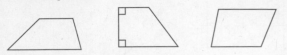

two-dimensional figure A figure with two dimensions, usually length and width.

Examples:

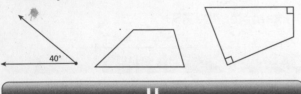

U

underestimate An estimate that is too small.

unit cube A cube with sides lengths of 1 unit.

1 unit
1 unit
1 unit

unit fraction A fraction with a numerator of 1. A unit fraction is one equal part of a whole.

Examples: $\frac{1}{3}$ and $\frac{1}{12}$

unsimplify Make an equivalent fraction by multiplying the numerator and denominator of a fraction by the same number. Unsimplifying makes more but smaller parts.

Example: Unsimplify $\frac{3}{4}$ by multiplying the numerator and denominator by 2.

$$\frac{3 \times 2}{4 \times 2} = \frac{6}{8}$$

V

variable A letter or other symbol used to stand for an unknown number in an algebraic expression.

volume A measure of the amount of space occupied by a solid figure. Volume is measured in cubic units.

W

word form The form of a number that uses words instead of digits.

Example: twelve and thirty-two hundredths

X

x-axis The horizontal axis of the coordinate plane.

x-coordinate The first number in an ordered pair, which represents a point's horizontal distance from the y-axis.

Example: The x-coordinate of the point represented by the ordered pair (3, 4) is 3.

Y

y-axis The vertical axis of the coordinate plane.

y-coordinate The second number in an ordered pair, which represents a point's vertical distance from the x-axis.

Example: The y-coordinate of the point represented by the ordered pair (3, 4) is 4.

California Common Core Standards for Mathematical Content

5.OA Operations and Algebraic Thinking

Write and interpret numerical expressions.

5.0A.1	Use parentheses, brackets, or braces in numerical expressions, and evaluate them with these symbols.	Unit 6 Lesson 8; Unit 7 Lessons 1, 2, 3, 4, 7
5.0A.2	Write simple expressions that record calculations with numbers, and interpret numerical expressions without evaluating them.	Unit 7 Lessons 1, 3, 4
5.0A.2.1	Express a whole number in the range 2–50 as a product of its prime factors.	Unit 7 Lesson 4

Analyze patterns and relationships.

5.0A.3	Generate two numerical patterns using two given rules. Identify apparent relationships between corresponding terms. Form ordered pairs consisting of corresponding terms from the two patterns, and graph the ordered pairs on a coordinate plane.	Unit 7 Lessons 4, 6

5.NBT Number and Operations in Base Ten

Understand the place value system.

5.NBT.1	Recognize that in a multi-digit number, a digit in one place represents 10 times as much as it represents in the place to its right and $\frac{1}{10}$ of what it represents in the place to its left.	Unit 2 Lessons 2, 3; Unit 4 Lessons 1, 3, 7, 9
5.NBT.2	Explain patterns in the number of zeros of the product when multiplying a number by powers of 10, and explain patterns in the placement of the decimal point when a decimal is multiplied or divided by a power of 10. Use whole-number exponents to denote powers of 10.	Unit 4 Lessons 1, 2, 6, 7, 9; Unit 5 Lessons 6, 7, 8
5.NBT.3	Read, write, and compare decimals to thousandths.	Unit 2 Lessons 1, 2, 3; Unit 4 Lesson 12
5.NBT.3a	Read and write decimals to thousandths using base-ten numerals, number names, and expanded form, e.g., $347.392 = 3 \times 100 + 4 \times 10 + 7 \times 1 + 3 \times (\frac{1}{10}) + 9 \times (\frac{1}{100}) + 2 \times (\frac{1}{1000})$.	Unit 2 Lessons 1, 2, 3
5.NBT.3b	Compare two decimals to thousandths based on meanings of the digits in each place, using >, =, and < symbols to record the results of comparisons.	Unit 2 Lessons 3, 9; Unit 4 Lesson 12; Unit 5 Lesson 10
5.NBT.4	Use place value understanding to round decimals to any place.	Unit 2 Lessons 8, 9; Unit 4 Lesson 10; Unit 6 Lesson 4

Perform operations with multi-digit whole numbers and with decimals to hundredths.

5.NBT.5	Fluently multiply multi-digit whole numbers using the standard algorithm.	Unit 4 Lessons 3, 4, 5, 8, 11, 12; Unit 5 Lesson 10; Unit 6 Lessons 2, 5, 6, 7, 8, 9
5.NBT.6	Find whole-number quotients of whole numbers with up to four-digit dividends and two-digit divisors, using strategies based on place value, the properties of operations, and/or the relationship between multiplication and division. Illustrate and explain the calculation by using equations, rectangular arrays, and/or area models.	Unit 5 Lessons 1, 2, 3, 4, 5, 9, 10; Unit 6 Lessons 2, 4, 6, 7, 9, 10
5.NBT.7	Add, subtract, multiply, and divide decimals to hundredths, using concrete models or drawings and strategies based on place value, properties of operations, and/or the relationship between addition and subtraction; relate the strategy to a written method and explain the reasoning used.	Unit 2 Lessons 4, 5, 6, 7, 10; Unit 4 Lessons 1, 6, 7, 8, 9, 10, 11, 12; Unit 5 Lessons 6, 7, 8, 9, 10, 11; Unit 6 Lessons 1, 2, 4, 6, 7, 8, 9, 11

5.NF Number and Operations–Fractions

Use equivalent fractions as a strategy to add and subtract fractions.

5.NF.1	Add and subtract fractions with unlike denominators (including mixed numbers) by replacing given fractions with equivalent fractions in such a way as to produce an equivalent sum or difference of fractions with like denominators.	Unit 1 Lessons 2, 3, 4, 5, 7, 8, 9, 10, 11, 12, 13; Unit 3 Lessons 7, 8, 13; Unit 6 Lesson 4
5.NF.2	Solve word problems involving addition and subtraction of fractions referring to the same whole, including cases of unlike denominators, e.g., by using visual fraction models or equations to represent the problem. Use benchmark fractions and number sense of fractions to estimate mentally and assess the reasonableness of answers.	Unit 1 Lessons 1, 6, 7, 8, 9, 10, 11, 12, 13; Unit 3 Lessons 7, 8, 13; Unit 6 Lessons 1, 4, 7, 8, 9, 10

Apply and extend previous understandings of multiplication and division to multiply and divide fractions.

5.NF.3	Interpret a fraction as division of the numerator by the denominator ($\frac{a}{b} = a \div b$). Solve word problems involving division of whole numbers leading to answers in the form of fractions or mixed numbers, e.g., by using visual fraction models or equations to represent the problem.	Unit 3 Lessons 10, 11, 13, 14; Unit 6 Lesson 11
5.NF.4	Apply and extend previous understandings of multiplication to multiply a fraction or whole number by a fraction.	Unit 3 Lessons 1, 2, 3, 4, 5, 6, 7, 8, 9, 10, 12, 13; Unit 6 Lesson 2
5.NF.4a	Interpret the product ($\frac{a}{b}$) × q as a parts of a partition of q into b equal parts; equivalently, as the result of a sequence of operations $a \times q \div b$.	Unit 3 Lessons 1, 2, 3, 4, 5, 7, 10; Unit 6 Lesson 3

5.NF.4b	Find the area of a rectangle with fractional side lengths by tiling it with unit squares of the appropriate unit fraction side lengths, and show that the area is the same as would be found by multiplying the side lengths. Multiply fractional side lengths to find areas of rectangles, and represent fraction products as rectangular areas.	Unit 3 Lessons 4, 6; Unit 6 Lesson 2; Unit 8 Lesson 8
5.NF.5	Interpret multiplication as scaling (resizing), by:	Unit 3 Lessons 1, 6, 7, 8, 9, 12, 13; Unit 4 Lesson 12; Unit 5 Lesson 10; Unit 6 Lesson 6
5.NF.5a	Comparing the size of a product to the size of one factor on the basis of the size of the other factor, without performing the indicated multiplication.	Unit 3 Lessons 6, 7, 8, 9, 12, 13, 14; Unit 4 Lesson 12; Unit 5 Lesson 10; Unit 6 Lesson 6
5.NF.5b	Explaining why multiplying a given number by a fraction greater than 1 results in a product greater than the given number (recognizing multiplication by whole numbers greater than 1 as a familiar case); explaining why multiplying a given number by a fraction less than 1 results in a product smaller than the given number; and relating the principle of fraction equivalence $\frac{a}{b} = \frac{(n \times a)}{(n \times b)}$ to the effect of multiplying $\frac{a}{b}$ by 1.	Unit 3 Lessons 1, 6, 7, 9, 12; Unit 4 Lesson 12; Unit 6 Lesson 6
5.NF.6	Solve real world problems involving multiplication of fractions and mixed numbers, e.g., by using visual fraction models or equations to represent the problem.	Unit 3 Lessons 1, 2, 3, 4, 5, 6, 7, 8, 9, 12, 13, 14; Unit 6 Lessons 2, 6, 8, 9, 10
5.NF.7	Apply and extend previous understandings of division to divide unit fractions by whole numbers and whole numbers by unit fractions.	Unit 3 Lessons 10, 11, 12, 13; Unit 6 Lesson 2
5.NF.7a	Interpret division of a unit fraction by a non-zero whole number, and compute such quotients.	Unit 3 Lessons 10, 11, 12, 13; Unit 6 Lesson 3
5.NF.7b	Interpret division of a whole number by a unit fraction, and compute such quotients.	Unit 3 Lessons 10, 11, 12, 13; Unit 6 Lesson 3
5.NF.7c	Solve real world problems involving division of unit fractions by non-zero whole numbers and division of whole numbers by unit fractions, e.g., by using visual fraction models and equations to represent the problem.	Unit 3 Lessons 10, 11, 12, 13, 14; Unit 6 Lessons 2, 6, 8, 10

5.MD Measurement and Data

Convert like measurement units within a given measurement system.

5.MD.1	Convert among different-sized standard measurement units within a given measurement system (e.g., convert 5 cm to 0.05 m), and use these conversions in solving multi-step, real world problems.	Unit 2 Lesson 4; Unit 8 Lessons 1, 2, 3, 4, 5, 6

Represent and interpret data.

5.MD.2	Make a line plot to display a data set of in fractions of a unit $(\frac{1}{2}, \frac{1}{4}, \frac{1}{8})$. Use operations on fractions for this grade to solve problems involving information presented in line plots.	Unit 1 Lesson 10; Unit 3 Lesson 13; Unit 8 Lesson 7

Geometric measurement: understand concepts of volume and relate volume to multiplication and to addition.

5.MD.3	Recognize volume as an attribute of solid figures and understand concepts of volume measurement.	Unit 8 Lessons 10, 17
5.MD.3a	A cube with side length 1 unit, called a "unit cube," is said to have "one cubic unit" of volume, and can be used to measure volume.	Unit 8 Lessons 9, 10
5.MD.3b	A solid figure which can be packed without gaps or overlaps using n unit cubes is said to have a volume of n cubic units.	Unit 8 Lessons 9, 10
5.MD.4	Measure volumes by counting unit cubes, using cubic cm, cubic in., cubic ft, and improvised units.	Unit 8 Lessons 9, 11
5.MD.5	Relate volume to the operations of multiplication and addition and solve real world and mathematical problems involving volume.	Unit 8 Lessons 13, 17
5.MD.5a	Find the volume of a right rectangular prism with whole-number side lengths by packing it with unit cubes, and show that the volume is the same as would be found by multiplying the edge lengths, equivalently by multiplying the height by the area of the base. Represent threefold whole-number products as volumes, e.g., to represent the associative property of multiplication.	Unit 8 Lessons 9, 11
5.MD.5b	Apply the formulas $V = l \times w \times h$ and $V = b \times h$ for rectangular prisms to find volumes of right rectangular prisms with whole number edge lengths in the context of solving real world and mathematical problems.	Unit 8 Lessons 11, 12, 13, 17
5.MD.5c	Recognize volume as additive. Find volumes of solid figures composed of two non-overlapping right rectangular prisms by adding the volumes of the non-overlapping parts, applying this technique to solve real world problems.	Unit 8 Lesson 13

Graph points on the coordinate plane to solve real-world and mathematical problems.

5.G.1	Use a pair of perpendicular number lines, called axes, to define a coordinate system, with the intersection of the lines (the origin) arranged to coincide with the 0 on each line and a given point in the plane located by using an ordered pair of numbers, called its coordinates.Understand that the first number indicates how far to travel from the origin in the direction of one axis, and the second number indicates how far to travel in the direction of the second axis, with the convention that the names of the two axes and the coordinates correspond (e.g., *x*-axis and *x*-coordinate, *y*-axis and *y*-coordinate).	Unit 7 Lessons 5, 6, 7
5.G.2	Represent real world and mathematical problems by graphing points in the first quadrant of the coordinate plane, and interpret coordinate values of points in the context of the situation.	Unit 7 Lessons 6, 7

Classify two-dimensional figures into categories based on their properties.

5.G.3	Understand that attributes belonging to a category of two-dimensional figures also belong to all subcategories of that category.	Unit 8 Lessons 14, 15, 16
5.G.4	Classify two-dimensional figures in a hierarchy based on properties.	Unit 8 Lessons 14, 15, 16

California Common Core Standards for Mathematical Practice

MP.1 Make sense of problems and persevere in solving them.

Mathematically proficient students start by explaining to themselves the meaning of a problem and looking for entry points to its solution. They analyze givens, constraints, relationships, and goals. They make conjectures about the form and meaning of the solution and plan a solution pathway rather than simply jumping into a solution attempt. They consider analogous problems, and try special cases and simpler forms of the original problem in order to gain insight into its solution. They monitor and evaluate their progress and change course if necessary. Older students might, depending on the context of the problem, transform algebraic expressions or change the viewing window on their graphing calculator to get the information they need. Mathematically proficient students can explain correspondences between equations, verbal descriptions, tables, and graphs or draw diagrams of important features and relationships, graph data, and search for regularity or trends. Younger students might rely on using concrete objects or pictures to help conceptualize and solve a problem. Mathematically proficient students check their answers to problems using a different method, and they continually ask themselves, "Does this make sense?" They can understand the approaches of others to solving complex problems and identify correspondences between different approaches.

Unit 1 Lessons 1, 7, 8, 9, 12, 13; Unit 2 Lessons 4, 6, 8, 9, 10; Unit 3 Lessons 1, 2, 3, 4, 5, 6, 7, 8, 9, 10, 11, 12, 13, 14; Unit 4 Lessons 1, 3, 6, 7, 8, 11, 12; Unit 5 Lessons 1, 2, 4, 6, 7, 8, 9, 10, 11; Unit 6 Lessons 1, 2, 4, 5, 6, 7, 8, 9, 10, 11; Unit 7 Lessons 3, 4, 6, 7; Unit 8 Lessons 1, 2, 3, 4, 5, 6, 11, 13, 15, 17

MP.2 Reason abstractly and quantitatively.

Mathematically proficient students make sense of quantities and their relationships in problem situations. They bring two complementary abilities to bear on problems involving quantitative relationships: the ability to *decontextualize*—to abstract a given situation and represent it symbolically and manipulate the representing symbols as if they have a life of their own, without necessarily attending to their referents—and the ability to *contextualize*, to pause as needed during the manipulation process in order to probe into the referents for the symbols involved. Quantitative reasoning entails habits of creating a coherent representation of the problem at hand; considering the units involved; attending to the meaning of quantities, not just how to compute them; and knowing and flexibly using different properties of operations and objects.

Unit 1 Lessons 1, 2, 3, 4, 5, 7, 8, 13; Unit 2 Lessons 1, 2, 3, 4, 5, 8, 10; Unit 3 Lessons 3, 4, 5, 6, 7, 8, 10, 11, 12, 14; Unit 4 Lessons 1, 3, 7, 9, 10, 11, 12; Unit 5 Lessons 1, 3, 7, 8, 9, 10, 11; Unit 6 Lessons 1, 2, 3, 5, 6, 11; Unit 7 Lessons 1, 4, 5, 6, 7; Unit 8 Lessons 1, 4, 5, 6, 10, 17

MP.3 Construct viable arguments and critique the reasoning of others.

Mathematically proficient students understand and use stated assumptions, definitions, and previously established results in constructing arguments. They make conjectures and build a logical progression of statements to explore the truth of their conjectures. They are able to analyze situations by breaking them into cases, and can recognize and use counterexamples. They justify their conclusions, communicate them to others, and respond to the arguments of others. They reason inductively about data, making plausible arguments that take into account the context from which the data arose. Mathematically proficient students are also able to compare the effectiveness of two plausible arguments, distinguish correct logic or reasoning from that which is flawed, and—if there is a flaw in an argument—explain what it is. Elementary students can construct arguments using concrete referents such as objects, drawings, diagrams, and actions. Such arguments can make sense and be correct, even though they are not generalized or made formal until later grades. Later, students learn to determine domains to which an argument applies. Students at all grades can listen or read the arguments of others, decide whether they make sense, and ask useful questions to clarify or improve the arguments.

Unit 1 Lessons 1, 2, 3, 4, 5, 6, 7, 8, 9, 10, 11, 12, 13; Unit 2 Lessons 1, 2, 3, 4, 5, 6, 7, 8, 9, 10; Unit 3 Lessons 1, 2, 3, 4, 5, 6, 7, 8, 9, 10, 11, 12, 13, 14; Unit 4 Lessons 1, 2, 3, 4, 6, 7, 8, 9, 10, 11, 12; Unit 5 Lessons 1, 2, 3, 4, 5, 6, 7, 8, 9, 10, 11; Unit 6 Lessons 1, 2, 3, 4, 5, 6, 7, 8, 9, 10, 11; Unit 7 Lessons 1, 2, 3, 4, 5, 6, 7; Unit 8 Lessons 1, 2, 3, 4, 5, 6, 7, 8, 9, 10, 11, 12, 13, 14, 15, 16, 17

MP.4 Model with mathematics.

Mathematically proficient students can apply the mathematics they know to solve problems arising in everyday life, society, and the workplace. In early grades, this might be as simple as writing an addition equation to describe a situation. In middle grades, a student might apply proportional reasoning to plan a school event or analyze a problem in the community. By high school, a student might use geometry to solve a design problem or use a function to describe how one quantity of interest depends on another. Mathematically proficient students who can apply what they know are comfortable making assumptions and approximations to simplify a complicated situation, realizing that these may need revision later. They are able to identify important quantities in a practical situation and map their relationships using such tools as diagrams, two-way tables, graphs, flowcharts and formulas. They can analyze those relationships mathematically to draw conclusions. They routinely interpret their mathematical results in the context of the situation and reflect on whether the results make sense, possibly improving the model if it has not served its purpose.

Unit 1 Lessons 1, 3, 5, 6, 7, 8, 9, 12, 13; Unit 2 Lessons 4, 9, 10; Unit 3 Lessons 1, 2, 4, 10, 11, 14; Unit 4 Lessons 1, 2, 3, 6, 12; Unit 5 Lessons 1, 2, 6, 11; Unit 6 Lessons 1, 2, 3, 4, 5, 6, 7, 8, 10, 11; Unit 7 Lessons 3, 6, 7; Unit 8 Lessons 7, 9, 10, 15, 17

MP.5 Use appropriate tools strategically.

Mathematically proficient students consider the available tools when solving a mathematical problem. These tools might include pencil and paper, concrete models, a ruler, a protractor, a calculator, a spreadsheet, a computer algebra system, a statistical package, or dynamic geometry software. Proficient students are sufficiently familiar with tools appropriate for their grade or course to make sound decisions about when each of these tools might be helpful, recognizing both the insight to be gained and their limitations. For example, mathematically proficient high school students analyze graphs of functions and solutions generated using a graphing calculator. They detect possible errors by strategically using estimation and other mathematical knowledge. When making mathematical models, they know that technology can enable them to visualize the results of varying assumptions, explore consequences, and compare predictions with data. Mathematically proficient students at various grade levels are able to identify relevant external mathematical resources, such as digital content located on a website, and use them to pose or solve problems. They are able to use technological tools to explore and deepen their understanding of concepts.

Unit 1 Lessons 1, 2, 3, 4, 5, 13; Unit 2 Lessons 2, 3, 4, 6, 8, 10; Unit 3 Lessons 3, 4, 10, 11, 14; Unit 4 Lessons 1, 12; Unit 5 Lessons 6, 11; Unit 6 Lessons 3, 11; Unit 7 Lessons 5, 6, 7; Unit 8 Lessons 7, 9, 11, 14, 15, 16, 17

MP.6 Attend to precision.

Mathematically proficient students try to communicate precisely to others. They try to use clear definitions in discussion with others and in their own reasoning. They state the meaning of the symbols they choose, including using the equal sign consistently and appropriately. They are careful about specifying units of measure, and labeling axes to clarify the correspondence with quantities in a problem. They calculate accurately and efficiently, express numerical answers with a degree of precision appropriate for the problem context. In the elementary grades, students give carefully formulated explanations to each other. By the time they reach high school they have learned to examine claims and make explicit use of definitions.

Unit 1 Lessons 1, 2, 3, 4, 5, 6, 7, 8, 9, 10, 11, 12, 13; Unit 2 Lessons 1, 2, 3, 4, 5, 6, 7, 8, 9, 10; Unit 3 Lessons 1, 2, 3, 4, 5, 6, 7, 8, 9, 10, 11, 12, 13, 14; Unit 4 Lessons 1, 2, 3, 4, 5, 6, 7, 8, 9, 10, 11, 12; Unit 5 Lessons 1, 2, 3, 4, 5, 6, 7, 8, 9, 10, 11; Unit 6 Lessons 1, 2, 3, 4, 5, 6, 7, 8, 9, 10, 11; Unit 7 Lessons 1, 2, 3, 4, 5, 6, 7; Unit 8 Lessons 1, 2, 3, 4, 5, 6, 7, 8, 9, 10, 11, 12, 13, 14, 15, 16, 17

MP.7 Look for and make use of structure.

Mathematically proficient students look closely to discern a pattern or structure. Young students, for example, might notice that three and seven more is the same amount as seven and three more, or they may sort a collection of shapes according to how many sides the shapes have. Later, students will see 7×8 equals the well remembered $7 \times 5 + 7 \times 3$, in preparation for learning about the distributive property. In the expression $x^2 + 9x + 14$, older students can see the 14 as 2×7 and the 9 as $2 + 7$. They recognize the significance of an existing line in a geometric figure and can use the strategy of drawing an auxiliary line for solving problems. They also can step back for an overview and shift perspective. They can see complicated things, such as some algebraic expressions, as single objects or as being composed of several objects. For example, they can see $5 - 3(x - y)^2$ as 5 minus a positive number times a square and use that to realize that its value cannot be more than 5 for any real numbers x and y.

Unit 1 Lessons 1, 2, 3, 4, 9, 10, 12, 13; Unit 2 Lessons 1, 3, 4, 7, 10; Unit 3 Lessons 1, 2, 4, 6, 7, 10, 14; Unit 4 Lessons 2, 4, 6, 7, 8, 9, 12; Unit 5 Lessons 1, 6, 8, 9, 11; Unit 6 Lessons 2, 4, 6, 7, 11; Unit 7 Lessons 2, 4, 5, 7; Unit 8 Lessons 1, 2, 5, 6, 9, 14, 15, 16, 17

MP.8 Look for and express regularity in repeated reasoning.

Mathematically proficient students notice if calculations are repeated, and look both for general methods and for shortcuts. Upper elementary students might notice when dividing 25 by 11 that they are repeating the same calculations over and over again, and conclude they have a repeating decimal. By paying attention to the calculation of slope as they repeatedly check whether points are on the line through $(1, 2)$ with slope 3, middle school students might abstract the equation $(y - 2)/(x - 1) = 3$. Noticing the regularity in the way terms cancel when expanding $(x - 1)(x + 1)$, $(x - 1)$ $(x^2 + x + 1)$, and $(x - 1)(x^3 + x^2 + x + 1)$ might lead them to the general formula for the sum of a geometric series. As they work to solve a problem, mathematically proficient students maintain oversight of the process, while attending to the details. They continually evaluate the reasonableness of their intermediate results.

Unit 1 Lessons 3, 4, 7, 8, 9, 10, 13; Unit 2 Lessons 1, 2, 3, 7, 8, 10; Unit 3 Lessons 2, 3, 4, 6, 7, 9, 10, 12, 13, 14; Unit 4 Lessons 1, 2, 6, 7, 8, 9, 11, 12; Unit 5 Lessons 1, 3, 6, 7, 10, 11; Unit 6 Lessons 4, 6, 11; Unit 7 Lessons 3, 4, 5, 7; Unit 8 Lessons 2, 3, 7, 8, 13, 17

Index

B

C

Index (continued)

plot points, 250–251, 253–254

real world, 254

x-axis and y-axis, 249–256

Coordinate Plane Poster. *See* **Manipulatives**

Counterexample, 295, 297

Cup, 275

Customary measurement. *See* **Measurement, customary**

D

Data

graph, 55–56

line plot, 24, 102, 279–280

Decimals

add, 47–48

compare, 44, 56

connect to fractions, 185

operations, 194

order and, 56

convert to fractions, 185

divide, 177–190, 193–196

equivalent, 43

estimate, 54

expanded form, 42

fractions and, 92, 185

graph, 55–56

multiply, 116–117, 131–145, 151–152, 181–182, 193–196

patterns in, 134

place values in, 40, 41, 187–188

powers of ten, 180, 181

read, 40

relate fractions and, 39–40, 185

parts of a whole, 39–40

relate to metric lengths, 45–46, 48

round, 53, 149

Secret Code Cards, 41–42D

subtract, 49–50

symmetry around ones place, 41–42D

tenths and hundredths, 39, 41–42D, 181–183

thousandths, 39, 41–42D, 116

word names for, 42A–42D

write, 40, 56

write fractions as, 39

zeros in the product, 134, 148

Denominator, 9–10, 19–20

common, 10, 12, 18, 22, 23

greatest common, 18

Difference. *See* **Subtraction**

Digit-by-Digit, 169–170, 175

Distributive Property, 51–52, 85, 123

Division

adjusting estimate, 169–170

check for reasonable answers, 192, 213

with decimals, 177–179, 181–196

decimals in, 177–190

drawings, 95, 211–212

equations, 209–210

estimation in, 167–170, 213

fractions in, 5–6, 97–102, 184

unit, 92–94

word problems with, 97

methods, 163, 184, 192

adjusted estimate, 169–170

digit-by-digit, 169–170, 175

expanded notation, 169–170, 175

of multidigit whole numbers, 163–166

by one-digit divisors, 163–166, 175, 177

real world situations, 96, 171–174, 176, 192

© Houghton Mifflin Harcourt Publishing Company

Index (continued)

G

N

O

P